Science Made Simple

Grade 2

Written by Vicky Shiotsu
Illustrated by Patty McCloskey

PHOTO CREDITS
page 1: Dunes photograph by Joe Lange
Cactus photograph by Eric Wunrow
page 4: Polar bears photograph by Joe Lange
page 7: Tarantula photograph by Eric Wunrow
page 54: Cracked mud photograph by Joe Lange

Notice! Copies of student pages may be reproduced by the classroom teacher for classroom use only, not for commercial resale. No part of this publication may be reproduced for storage in a retrieval system, or transmitted in any form or by any means–electronic, mechanical, recording, etc.–without the prior written permission of the publisher. Reproduction of these materials for an entire school or school system is strictly prohibited.

FS-23212 Science Made Simple Grade 2
All rights reserved–Printed in the U.S.A.
Copyright © 1997 Frank Schaffer Publications
23740 Hawthorne Blvd.
Torrance, CA 90505

Introduction

Children have an inherent drive to find out about the world around them. They are curious about what they see or experience, and they often display their interest by asking questions.

How do birds fly?

Do fish breathe?

Why is there a rainbow in the sky?

How come things fall down?

These and other questions are children's attempts to make sense of their environment.

Asking questions is an important part of learning and discovery. *Science Made Simple Grade 2* is designed to help teachers plan a science program that builds upon children's natural inquisitiveness about their world. The numerous hands-on activities in this book encourage children to make observations, ask questions, test ideas, and share results. As you lead the children through the various activities, you can stimulate their thinking by asking thought-provoking questions (suggestions are presented throughout the book) and by allowing the students to branch out into their own investigations. For example, your students may wish to read some of the recommended literature selections or they may want to create new experiments by adapting the ones described in this book.

Science Made Simple Grade 2 can be used alone or as an integral part of any science program. The book is divided into three sections: Life Science, Physical Science, and Earth Science. Each section covers a variety of topics that are interesting, challenging, and age-appropriate. The activities in each section may be introduced sequentially as they appear in the book or in random order.

Science is a subject that encourages exploration, experimentation, and discovery. It is hoped that as you implement the ideas in this book, your students will become better observers, questioners, and problem-solvers. It is also hoped that as your students conduct various investigations, they will enjoy science as a fun, rewarding, and meaningful part of their school experience.

Life Science

Children are fascinated with the living world and are naturally curious about the plants and animals that inhabit the Earth. As children are introduced to various life forms—both past and present—they will begin to discover how all living things are wonderfully suited to their environment. As children reflect on how they themselves react to their environment (dressing warmly in cold weather or wearing sunglasses in bright light), they begin to understand that all living things interact with their surroundings and that some life forms—namely, animals and people—rely on their senses to learn about changes in their world.

CONCEPTS

The ideas and activities presented in this section will help children explore the following concepts:

- Every living thing is suited to its environment.
- Living things have special characteristics that help them survive in their environment.
- Different kinds of plants and animals lived long ago. They became extinct when they could not adapt to changes in the environment.
- Senses help people and animals gain information about their environment.

LITERATURE RESOURCES

These appealing resources will help children learn more about living things.

Exploring Deserts by Barbara J. Behm and Veronica Bonar (Gareth Stevens Publishing, 1994). This colorful book examines the desert and the plants and animals that live there. Other titles in the series include *Exploring Mountains*, *Exploring Forests*, and *Exploring Seashores*.

Questions and Answers About Polar Animals by Michael Chinery (Kingfisher Books, 1994). This resource contains fascinating facts and colorful pictures.

The Very First Dinosaurs by Dougal Dixon (Gareth Stevens Children's Books, 1989). This easy-to-read book is part of a series that introduces children to dinosaurs. A list of "Fun Facts" is included.

Dinosaurs by Gallimard Jeunesse, et al. (Scholastic, 1993). This beautifully illustrated book has plastic overlays that let children change scenes and read hidden text.

Floratorium by Joanne Oppenheim (Bantam Books, 1994). Readers take a tour through a museum that presents different regions of the Earth and their varied plant life.

Your Amazing Senses by Ron and Atie van der Meer (Aladdin Books, 1987). Puzzles, games, scratch-and-sniff stickers, optical illusions, and more make up this fun, interactive book.

LIFE SCIENCE

• Living Things and Their Environment • Living Things of Long Ago • The Senses •

Living Things and Their Environment

Plants and animals live in many different kinds of environments. In order to survive, they must adapt to the conditions that distinguish where they live. Plants and animals that live in the far north, for example, must be able to withstand freezing temperatures; those that live in the desert must be able to go for long periods without water. As your students study how plants and animals live, they will discover that all living organisms have special characteristics that enable them to survive in their specific environments.

MANY KINDS OF ENVIRONMENT

Class Activity

Show your class pictures of different environments such as a polar region, a desert, and a rain forest. Discuss the characteristics of each environment and brainstorm the types of plants and animals that might live there. Ask what traits a plant or animal would need in order to survive in the far north, in the desert, and so on. Guide the class into seeing that the type of environment determines what kinds of plants or animals live there. Explain that places that have warm climates and plenty of water support many kinds of species; places that are extremely cold or hot have fewer varieties because there are not as many plants and animals that can survive such conditions.

Next, divide the class into small groups and assign each group one of the following environments: desert, mountain, rain forest, Arctic, forest (or woodland), ocean. Then let the children look through library books and encyclopedias to research what plants and animals are found in the various environments. Have the members of each group make a picture chart or a mural showing what they found out.

WHERE DO THEY LIVE?

Class Activity

Discuss with the class the fact that every animal is specially suited to the type of environment in which it lives. Then give each student a copy of *Where Do They Live?* (page 3). After the children complete the page, discuss the different features each animal has. Next, challenge each student to write another set of clues for a different animal; tell the children that their clues should include information about how the animal is suited to its environment. Then let the students read their clues to the class while the rest of the children try to guess what animal is being described.

(Answers to page 3: camel–desert; polar bear–Arctic; bighorn sheep–mountain; sloth–rain forest; musk ox–Arctic; spider monkey–rain forest; fennec fox–desert; ibex–mountain)

Name _____

Activity Sheet

Where Do They Live?

Read about the animals below. Guess where each one lives. Write **desert**, **mountain**, **Arctic**, or **rain forest**.

1. The camel has a thick hide that protects it from the sun. It can go for days without water.

_____

5. The musk ox has a long, shaggy coat that protects it from freezing temperatures.

_____

2. The polar bear's thick layers of fat under its skin keep it warm. Its rough paws keep it from slipping on ice.

_____

6. The spider monkey moves through trees by using its arms to swing from branch to branch.

_____

3. The bighorn sheep is a good climber. Its hooves help it to hold on to rocks.

_____

7. The fennec fox has large ears that let heat escape. This helps keep it cool.

_____

4. The sloth hangs upside down in trees. Its fur grows in such a way that rain runs off it easily.

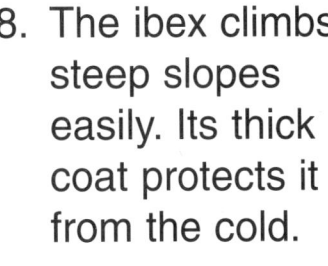

_____

8. The ibex climbs steep slopes easily. Its thick coat protects it from the cold.

_____

PLANTS AND ANIMALS WHERE I LIVE

Class Activity

Have the students describe the type of environment they live in. Ask the following types of questions to guide their thinking: *Are the summers hot? Are the winters cold or mild? Do we live near the ocean? Are there mountains nearby? Is the land mostly flat? Do you think the ground here is good for growing plants?* Then ask your students about the kinds of plants and animals they have seen in their neighborhood, and list their responses on the chalkboard. Discuss the fact that many kinds of plants and animals are often found in one area.

Next give students copies of *Plants Where I Live* and *Animals Where I Live* (pages 5 and 6) for a homework assignment. Instruct the children to search their neighborhood for various types of plants and animals, and have them draw pictures or write names to indicate what they discover. Afterwards, let your students share their findings with the class.

Art Project

What's Wrong?

Cut out a picture of a polar bear and glue it onto a desert scene. Show the picture to the class and ask the children what is wrong. Elicit from the students the fact that the polar bear is not in its natural environment. Ask the students how the bear might be feeling. (hot, uncomfortable) Guide the class into seeing that the polar bear's thick fur is suitable for a cold, icy region but unsuitable for a desert environment.

Next, let the students make their own "What's Wrong?" pictures. Give each child a sheet of drawing paper and have him or her draw a picture of a particular environment. Then have the student add an animal that is out of place in such an environment. (The children may draw their animals or glue on pictures cut from magazines or old calendars.) Afterwards, have each student show his or her picture to the class as the rest of the children try to decide what kind of environment is best for the animal.

Name _____

Plants Where I Live

Look for plants near where you live.
Write their names or draw their pictures below.

| Trees or Bushes | Grasses or Weeds |

Plants in My Neighborhood

| Flowers | Other Kinds of Plants |

Name _____

Activity Sheet

Animals Where I Live

Look for animals near where you live.
Write their names or draw their pictures below.

| Insects | Birds |

Animals in My Neighborhood

| Mammals (animals with fur or hair) | Other Kinds of Animals |

LIVING IN THE DESERT

Show your students pictures of deserts. Discuss the fact that desert plants and animals have learned to adapt to their harsh environment. Then try the following activities with your class:

WHAT HELPS A CACTUS SURVIVE?

Class Activity

Bring a small cactus for your students to examine. Point out the following features:

- **Long Roots**—The cactus has very long roots for collecting water from the ground.
- **Thick Stems**—The cactus has thick stems for storing water. These stems swell as more and more water is taken in.
- **Waxy Skin**—The waxy skin keeps water from evaporating. (You may wish to explain that when heated, water changes into gas and becomes part of the air.)
- **Spines**—Spines protect the cactus from animals that might want to eat it.

WHY DON'T DESERT PLANTS HAVE BROAD, FLAT LEAVES?

Class Activity

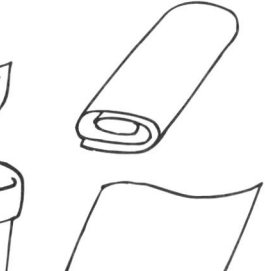

Have your students compare a broad-leafed houseplant and a cactus. Point out that the houseplant has thin stems and broad, flat leaves while the cactus has thick stems and no leaves. Then do this demonstration to illustrate why desert plants do not have broad, flat leaves.

Wet two sheets of paper by putting them under the faucet or by dipping them in a bowl of water. Lay one paper flat and roll up the other. Leave the papers in a warm place for one hour. The students will find that the flat, thin paper dries more quickly than the thick, rolled-up one. Tell the class that broad, flat leaves would cause a desert plant to lose water quickly; instead, many desert plants have no leaves or very small ones.

LIVING UNDERGROUND

Group Experiment

Tell your class that small desert animals such as insects and lizards live in the ground during the day. Then have your students do this experiment to find out why.

Divide the class into small groups and give each group copies of the experiment card and record sheet (pages 8 and 9). Take the students outdoors where they can scoop up pails of dirt and do the experiment. Afterwards, discuss the results with the class. (The dirt at the bottom of the pail is cooler than the dirt at the top.) Explain that desert animals stay underground during the day because it is cooler there and that they come out to feed at night.

© FS-23212 Science Made Simple • © Frank Schaffer Publications, Inc.

Name _____

Experiment

Living Underground

Question:
Why do some desert animals live underground?

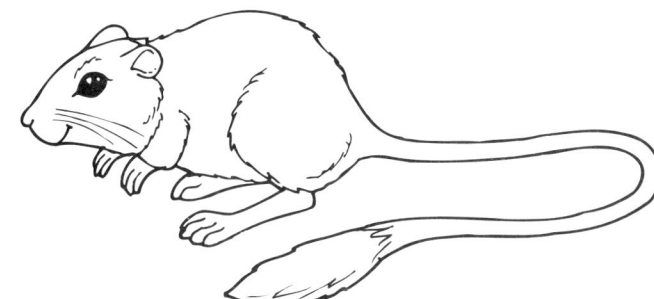

Prediction:
Write what you think on the record sheet.

Materials:
toy pail
dirt
trowel
craft stick
two thermometers

Directions:
1. Fill a pail with dirt. Set it in the sun for one hour.
2. Feel the dirt at the top of the pail. Then dig a hole in the dirt with a stick. Feel the dirt at the bottom of the pail.
3. Put a thermometer in the hole. Measure the temperature of the dirt at the bottom of the pail.
4. Get another thermometer. Measure the temperature of the dirt at the top of the pail.

Results:
Describe your results on the record sheet.

Conclusion:
Why do some desert animals live underground? Write your answer on the record sheet.

Name _____

Record Sheet

Living Underground

Question:
Why do some desert animals live underground?

Prediction:
Write what you think is the answer.

_____
_____
_____

Results:
How did the dirt at the top of the pail feel?
_____

How did the dirt at the bottom of the pail feel?
_____

Write the temperature of the dirt:

at the top of the pail _____   at the bottom of the pail _____

Conclusion:
Why do you think some desert animals live underground during the day?

_____
_____
_____

© FS-23212 Science Made Simple ▪ © Frank Schaffer Publications, Inc.

LIVING IN COLD PLACES

Show your class pictures of the Arctic and Antarctic regions. Point out these areas on a globe and tell your students that these regions are the coldest places on Earth. Then do the following activities to illustrate some of the ways plants and animals have adapted to their polar environments.

WHAT HELPS PLANTS SURVIVE IN POLAR REGIONS?

Class Activity

Display library books that feature pictures of plants that grow in the polar regions. Have the students notice that none of the plants are very tall. Tell them that these plants grow close to the ground where the air is warmer and where there is protection from freezing winds.

Next call on a student to stand in front of the class. Call on a group of five students to stand in a huddle away from the first student. Have the class imagine that the room is cold and snowy, and that icy winds are blowing. Ask who would stay warmer—the lone student or the group of five. After the children give their responses, tell them that the five students huddled together would stay warmer bcause they would be able to trap the warmer air surrounding their bodies. Explain that in a similar fashion, plants of the polar regions grow in clumps for protection against the cold.

THICK COATS OF FUR

Class Experiment

Display pictures of polar animals that have thick coats of fur or hair. (musk ox, polar bear, arctic fox, arctic hare) Then do this demonstration to show how thick coats protect animals from the cold.

Pour hot (not boiling) water into two mugs. Measure the temperature of the water in each mug and record it on the chalkboard. Cover one mug with a thick woolen sock. Wait 10 minutes and take the water temperature again in each mug. Continue recording the temperature every 10 minutes for an hour.

Your class will see that the water in the uncovered mug cools more quickly. Explain that the heat from the water escapes into the air. The woolen sock, however, traps the heat from the water, keeping it hotter longer. Similarly, the coats of polar animals trap the heat from their bodies and helps keep them warm.

BLUBBER FOR WARMTH

Class Experiment

Tell your students that penguins, seals, and other polar animals have a thick layer of blubber (fat). Have them do this activity to find out how blubber keeps animals warm.

Give the following instructions: Get two paper cups and two thermometers. Fill one cup half full of shortening. Put a thermometer into the shortening. Put the other thermometer into the empty cup. Record the temperature in each cup. Put the cups in the freezer for 30 minutes, recording the temperature every 10 minutes.

Your students will find that the temperature in the empty cup drops more quickly than the temperature in the cup of shortening; this is because the shortening helps to keep in the warmer air. In like manner, blubber protects the animals from the cold by slowing down the loss of body heat.

Living Things of Long Ago

At various times in the history of the Earth, the environment changed dramatically. For example, land masses moved, seas expanded and then shrank, and the climate shifted from warm to cold temperatures. As the environment changed, the types of plants and animals that existed changed, too. Some could not adjust to the changes in the environment and died. Others were able to adapt to the new conditions and survived. Many of the plants and animals we see today are very different from those that existed long ago.

COMPARING LENGTHS — Group Activity

Tell the class that although many dinosaurs were enormous in size, some were no larger than chickens. Then give each student a copy of *Comparing Lengths* (page 13) and do the following measurement activity.

Divide the class into small groups. Give each group several sheets of graph paper marked in one-inch squares. Tell the class to pretend that each inch represents one foot. Then have the children cut out strips of paper to show the sizes of the dinosaurs. (Examples: 2 inches = 2 feet; 6 inches = 6 feet, and so on) Have the children tape strips together to show longer lengths. Finally, have the students glue their strips onto butcher paper.

Days of the Dinosaurs — Art Project

Show your class several library books that feature dinosaurs. Tell the students that dinosaurs lived millions of years ago. Explain that these creatures lived at a time when the Earth's landscape and climate were quite different from what they are today.

Next, give each child a copy of *Days of the Dinosaurs* (page 12). Discuss the pictures and have the students compare the appearance of dinosaurs with that of modern-day animals.

Afterwards, give each child a deep box (such as a shoebox) for making a diorama. Instruct the students to color the dinosaurs and cut them out. Then have them research what the Earth looked like long ago and have them paint a prehistoric scene inside their boxes. (At the beginning of the dinosaur age, plant life consisted mostly of ferns, mosses, and trees. Later flowering plants appeared.) Let the students add grass, leaves, rocks, and other items to their scenes. Finally, have each student glue his or her dinosaurs so that they stand up inside the box.

© FS-23212 Science Made Simple ▪ © Frank Schaffer Publications, Inc.

Days of the Dinosaurs

Color the dinosaurs and cut them out. Make a scene to show what the Earth looked like long ago.

Comparing Lengths

Dinosaurs came in many sizes.

   Compsognathus   about 2 feet long

   Protoceratops   about 6 feet long

   Stegosaurus   about 25 feet long

   Triceratops   about 30 feet long

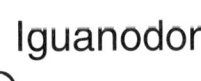   Iguanodon   about 35 feet long

Tyrannosaurus Rex   about 50 feet long

   Diplodocus   about 85 feet long

A GALLERY OF PREHISTORIC ANIMALS

Class Activity

Show pictures of prehistoric animals to your class. (Philip Steele's Extinct series published by Franklin Watts is a colorful resource for students.) Tell the class that prehistoric creatures lived millions of years ago and that they included dinosaurs, toothed birds, and armored fish. Explain that some animals, like the mammoth, resembled present-day animals; others were unlike any animals alive today.

Next, tell your students that they will be making a picture gallery to show what some prehistoric animals looked like. Then let the children browse through library books and other resources, and have each child choose one animal to illustrate. After the drawings are completed, have students write brief descriptions of their animals. Display the work on a bulletin board or in a hallway.

ANIMALS THEN AND NOW

Class Activity

Show pictures of prehistoric animals to your class. Discuss how these animals were very different from the animals that are alive today. (Examples: Many were much larger than today's animals; some had unusual body features.)

Next, tell the class that although prehistoric animals may seem strange and fantastic to us, they were in some ways quite similar. For example, creatures that were meat-eaters had sharp claws and teeth for capturing and killing their prey, just as present-day animal hunters do. Some plant-eating dinosaurs had long necks for feeding from the treetops—a feature characteristic of the modern giraffe.

Afterwards, give your students copies of *Animals Then and Now* (page 15). Instruct the children to decide what modern-day animals have traits similar to the prehistoric animals shown, and have the students draw pictures of their choices. Let your students share their work with the class.

Name _____

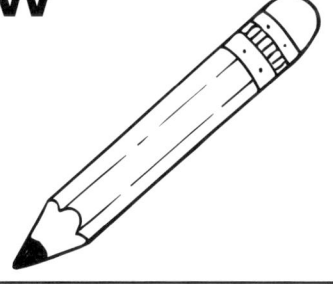

Activity Sheet

Animals Then and Now

Read about some prehistoric animals below. Then think about animals that are alive today that have something in common with these creatures. Draw their pictures.

 **The saber-toothed cat** had sharp teeth that looked like sabers (curved swords).	Draw an animal that has sharp teeth.
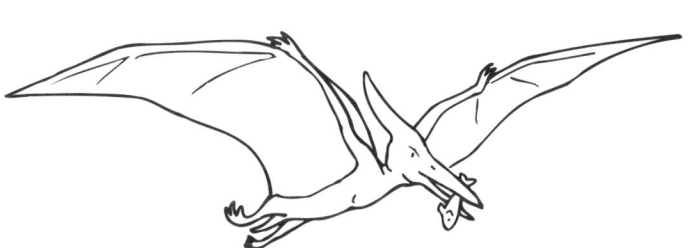 **The pteranodon** was a flying reptile. It ate fish.	Draw a flying animal that eats fish.
 **Apatosaurus** was a gigantic dinosaur with a long neck.	Draw an animal that has a long neck.

OUTLINES IN STONE

Class Activity

Tell your class that fossils have helped scientists learn about prehistoric times. Explain that some fossils are the remains of plants or animals that have been preserved in rock form. Then do this simple activity to demonstrate how fossils can reveal information about living things of long ago.

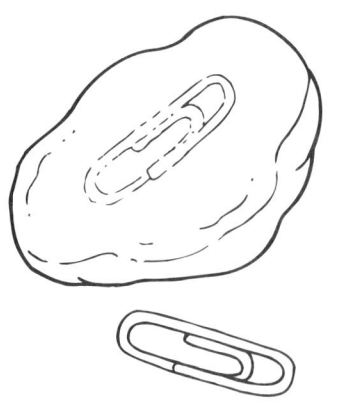

Get a ball of modeling clay and mold it into an oval shape. Next, press a paper clip into the clay. Pull out the paper clip and show your class the impression that is left behind. Tell your students that in some fossils the outlines of plants or animals are visible. Explain that these fossils formed when a plant or animal was buried in mud; later, the mud turned to stone after being covered and pressed by new layers of mud. The plant or animal parts eventually decayed, leaving an outline behind; these outlines (impressions) help scientists understand what prehistoric plants and animals looked like.

WHAT MADE THE TRACKS?

Class Activity

Tell the class that some fossils were formed from the tracks of prehistoric animals. These tracks were made when the animals walked across soft ground. The tracks dried and hardened in the sun and were later buried by mud or sand; over time, the tracks turned into stone.

Explain that tracks give important clues about the animals that made them. For example, the tracks may indicate an animal's size or appearance, or reveal information about how it traveled. Then challenge your students with this guessing game in which they look for clues in "tracks."

First, give every child a ball of modeling clay, and have the students shape their clay to look like a thick pancake. Next, have each student choose a classroom object for making tracks in the clay. (Examples: pencil, paper clip, brad fastener, ruler, lids of glue sticks) Then have the students make a set of tracks; the prints may be made by pressing the entire object into the clay or by inserting only the tip or edge of the object. Afterwards, display the tracks along a shelf and number them. Let the students test their observation skills as they write what object they think made each set of tracks.

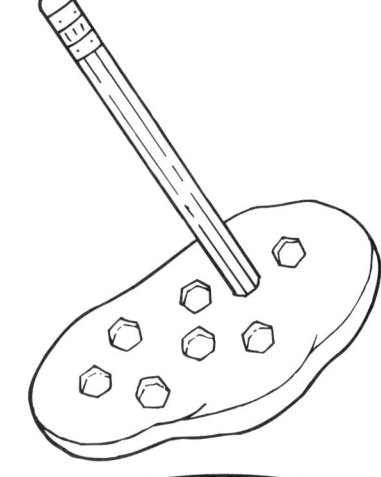

MAKE A FOSSIL

Group Activity

Your students will enjoy making their own "fossils." To begin, divide the class into groups of four, and give each group a copy of *A Fossil Recipe* (page 17). Then let the students make the modeling dough according to the directions. Afterwards, instruct the children to press small leaves or shells into the dough; have them carefully lift the leaves or shells to see the impressions left behind. (A toothpick may help lift the leaf off the dough more easily.) Leave the "fossils" on a sheet of wax paper and allow them to dry for three or four days. (Place unused dough in a plastic bag and store it in the refrigerator.)

Name _____

Activity Sheet

A Fossil Recipe

You can make your own "fossils" with this modeling dough recipe.

1. In a bowl, mix the following:

    1 cup flour

    ⅓ cup salt

    1 ½ tablespoons cream of tartar

    1 ½ tablespoons cooking oil

2. Add ⅓ cup of water. Mix well.

    Add more flour or water as needed.

    The mixture will feel like play dough.

3. Divide the dough into four balls. Use one ball for each fossil.

4. For the fossil, flatten a ball of dough into an oval.

    Press a small leaf or shell into the dough.

    Then gently pull out the leaf or shell.

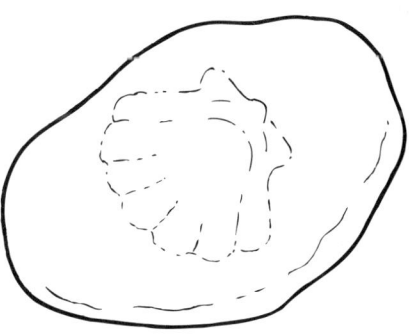

5. Let the fossil dry for three or four days.

    Don't forget to turn it over so that its back side will dry.

WHY DID PREHISTORIC ANIMALS DISAPPEAR?

Class Activity

Discuss with the students the fact that prehistoric animals became extinct (died out) many years ago. Explain that scientists do not know exactly why this happened, but that they have several theories (ideas):

- The climate got colder. Some prehistoric animals could not adapt to the change and died.

- Some plants died because of changes in the Earth (such as colder temperatures and less sunlight). Plant-eating animals died because their source of food was gone. Meat-eating animals died when there were no plant-eaters left.

- Some animals died because of disease.

Tell the class that today there are some animals that are in danger of becoming extinct, too. Add that these animals are endangered not because of changes created by nature but because of changes caused by people. Explain that these changes include the overhunting of certain animals and the destruction of animal habitats (homes). Tell your students that some people are working to prevent endangered animals from becoming extinct and that many have succeeded in their efforts. Then have your students imagine that they have been transported back to prehistoric times. Have the children write what steps they would take to help save the animals from the cold, from lack of food, and from disease.

WHAT IF?

Class Activity

Read Bernard Most's *If the Dinosaurs Came Back* (Harcourt Brace Jovanovich, 1978) to your class. This delightful book describes some ways people's lives could be made more pleasant if the dinosaurs came back. (For example, the author suggests that dinosaurs could give people a ride to work or that they could help trim lawns.) As you read the humorous story, your students will be enthralled by the book's simple, bold drawings.

After reading the book to the class, have your students make their own version of the story. Have each child write a page beginning with the phrase *If the dinosaurs came back . . . .* After the students illustrate their sentences, bind their pages together into a book for the classroom library.

The Senses

People and animals rely on their senses to gain information about what is happening around them. Through the senses of sight, sound, touch, smell, and taste, information is sent to the brain, allowing the body to respond appropriately in a given situation. For example, a person or an animal who sees a car approaching in a dangerous manner will try to move out of the way. As you give your students opportunities to learn about how their senses work, they will begin to see how senses provide the link between themselves and their environment.

SEEING AND DOING

Have your students brainstorm different activities that depend on the sense of sight, and list the suggestions on a sheet of chart paper. (Examples: reading, writing, watching TV, playing baseball, mowing the lawn) Discuss the fact that the sense of sight helps people observe things, learn new skills, do chores, and enjoy certain pastimes. Then have the students look at their list and identify which activities are related to work and which ones are associated with fun and relaxation. Have the students circle the work-related activities in red and the other activities in blue.

OUR AMAZING EYES · Class Experiment

Have the students point out what part of our bodies helps us see. (the eyes) Tell the class that the eye is an amazing organ (a part of a body that does a particular job). Explain that the eye can see things far away, such as a plane in the sky; it can also see things that are very small, such as grains of sand. Then let the students try this activity to see how carefully they can observe their eyes.

First give each child a mirror and a sheet of paper. Then instruct the students to look at one of their eyes and to draw it as accurately as they can. Later, draw an eye on the chalkboard and have the students compare your drawing to theirs. See if the children have noted the following:

eyelid—protects the front part of the eye; will blink if there is a sudden movement in front of the eye

eyelashes—protect the eye from dust and other particles that might enter the eye

sclera—the white part of the eye

iris—the colored disk in the eye

pupil—the dark circle in the center of the iris; it controls the amount of light that enters the eye

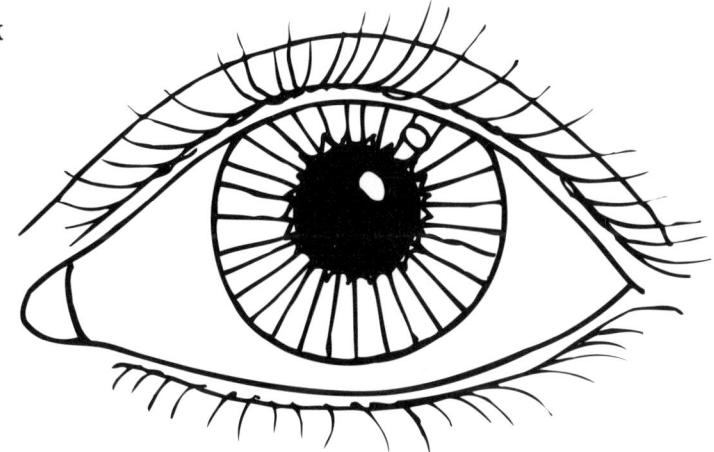

SEEING WITH TWO EYES

Ask the students why they have two eyes instead of one. Then let them try this activity to find out.

Instruct each child to place a small object on his or her desk, such as a pencil or an eraser. Next, have the student focus on the object with one eye closed; then have him or her look at the object with the other eye closed. The object looks as if it had moved slightly.

Explain that each eye sees at a slightly different angle. When we look at an object, the brain receives two different views from our eyes; the brain then puts the "pictures" together so that we see only one image. Tell the class that seeing with two eyes allows us to see an object as having thickness and form, and that we are also better able to judge how far away an object is than if we had only one eye.

HOLES IN OUR HANDS

See if your students can "produce" holes in their hands with this activity.

First, provide each child with a paper towel tube. Then give the following instructions: *Keep both eyes closed. With one hand hold the tube up to one eye. Hold up your other hand in front of the other eye, with your palm facing toward you. Position the hand so that it is even with the end of the tube. Slowly bring your hand toward you.*

Each child will see a hole in the middle of his or her hand. Explain that this happens because each eye sees a different image; one eye sees a circular view and the other a hand. The brain puts the two images together, causing the circular view (hole) to look as if it is in the middle of the hand.

FOOLING YOUR EYES

This project demonstrates how our senses can sometimes be fooled.

Reproduce *Fooling Your Eyes* (page 21) onto tagboard, and give a copy to each child. Have the students color the pictures, using the same color for the water in the bowl and the water around the fish. Tell the children to leave an uncolored border around the water that surrounds the fish.

Next, have the students cut out the boxes. Instruct each child to tape a pencil on the back of one picture and to glue the two pictures together back to back. Have the students spin their pictures back and forth. The fish looks as if it is in the bowl.

The illusion occurs because the brain continues to see an image for a brief time after the image has disappeared. When the students spin their pictures back and forth quickly, they see both bowl and the fish at the same time, making it appear as if the fish is in the bowl.

Name _____

Fooling Your Eyes

OUR EYES HELP US RESPOND

Discuss with the class the fact that our sense of sight helps us respond to the world around us. These responses often result in an action or a feeling. Then have the students write what they would do or how they would feel in the following situations:

- You see a friend walking toward you at school.
- You read a funny joke in a book.
- You see a scary monster in a movie.
- Just before going out, you see that it has started to rain.
- You see a beautiful sunset.
- You see a friend throwing you a baseball.

A REACTION TEST

Ask the students what a driver might do if he or she sees a person or an object appear suddenly in his or her path. Elicit from the class that the driver might brake suddenly or try to steer the car around the obstruction. Tell the class that a fast reaction is needed in this situation in order to avoid an accident.

Review with the students the fact that information about our surroundings is picked up by our senses; our senses then send messages to our brain, which makes a decision about how we should act. Tell the students that, as in the example of the driver, a quick reaction is often needed in dangerous situations. Then let them do the following activity to check how quickly they can act on their senses.

First, divide the class into pairs, and give each pair a ruler. Then instruct one student to hold the one-inch end of the ruler and suspend the opposite end between his or her partner's thumb and forefinger. Next have the student drop the ruler without warning, and have his or her partner try to catch it by closing his or her thumb and forefinger. Tell the students that the higher the number, the quicker is their reaction.

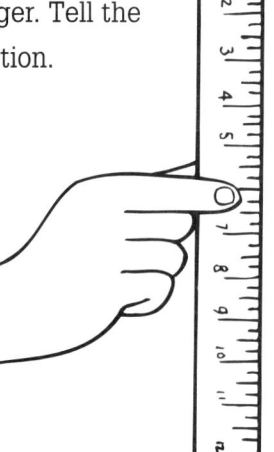

Let the students try the reaction test several times, giving each partner a chance to improve his or her performance. Ask how many students were able to speed up their reaction time with practice.

HOW OUR HEARING HELPS US — Group Activity

Divide the class into three groups and give each group a sheet of chart paper. Then assign each group one of the following titles to write on its paper: *People Hear and Have Fun, People Hear and Do Work, People Hear and Keep Safe*. Then have the students write examples of situations or activities in which people's ability to hear allows them to have fun, to do work, or to keep safe.

Examples:

Have Fun—People can listen to the radio, talk with a friend on the phone, watch a puppet show, sing along with a tape recording, dance to music, and play an instrument in a band.

Do Work—People can pilot a plane and talk with the control tower, tune a piano, work as a radio disc jockey or a telephone operator, and perform as a musician.

Keep Safe—People are able to respond to fire alarms, ambulance sirens, car horns, train whistles, and other sound signals; they can get on the phone and call for help if they hear suspicious noises outside their homes or if they are in trouble.

After the students have completed their suggestions, have the members of each group decorate their chart by illustrating some of the ideas. Later, let the students share their work with the class.

SOUND WAVES — Class Activity

This simple demonstration illustrates how sound reaches our ears.

First, call on a student to hold one end of a rope while you hold the other end. Then quickly move your end of the rope up and down. Your class will see that the movement travels along the rope in waves. Point out that when you move one end of the rope, the movement passes on from one part of the rope to the next until it has traveled to the other end.

Explain that this is the way sound travels through the air. Tell the class that sounds are caused by vibrations (quick movements) in the air; the vibrations travel in waves to our ears, and our brain interprets them as sound.

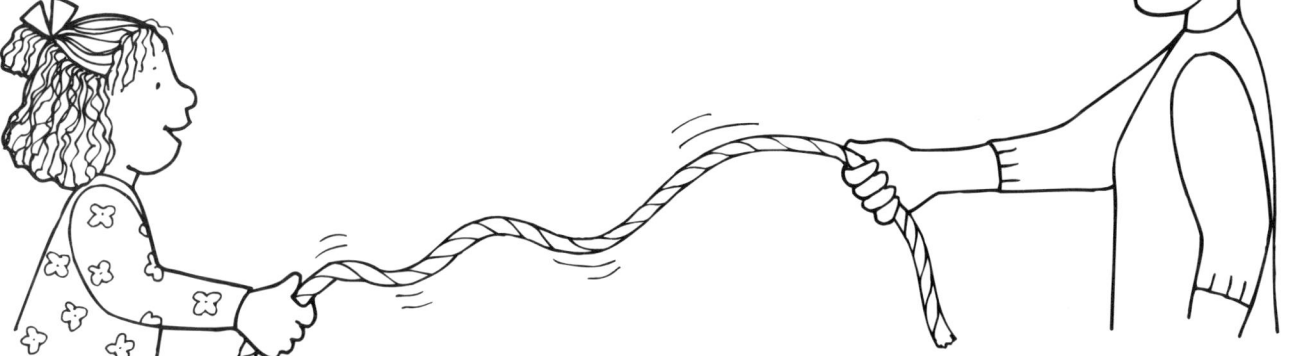

HEARING WITH TWO EARS — Class Activity

Have your class do this activity to discover why two ears are better than one.

Sit a student in a chair and blindfold him or her. Next, call on six students to stand around the blindfolded student, each holding two pencils. Point to a student and have the child tap his pencils together. Ask the blindfolded child to point toward the source of the sound. Continue signaling to the students one at a time, having them tap their pencils while the blindfolded child tries to determine the sound source.

Next, instruct the blindfolded child to cover one ear with his or her hand. Then repeat the activity described above. Your students will see that when one ear is covered, it is more difficult to tell where the sound is coming from. If you wish, continue the activity with different groups of children.

Later, tell the students that two ears allow us to figure out from which direction a sound is coming. Explain that when a sound comes from one side of us, it reaches one ear faster than it does the other. This time difference lets us tell the direction of the sound. Add that if the sound is directly in front of us, behind us, or above us, it is harder to determine its source. Covering one ear makes it even more difficult to identify where a sound is coming from.

HEARING THROUGH LIQUIDS AND SOLIDS — Group Experiment

Ask your students who are swimmers if they have been able to hear while swimming underwater. If they answer yes, ask them to describe what sounds they have heard. Tell the class that we can hear underwater because sound waves travel through water as well as through air.

Next, ask the students if they think that sounds travel through solids. Then let them do this activity to find out. Divide the class into pairs and give each pair a copy of *Listening Through Solids* (page 25). After the students complete the activity, they will discover that they can hear their partners' tapping better when they put an ear to their desks rather than when they sit up and listen to the sound.

Explain that sound travels through solids. In fact, sound waves travel better through wood than through air. That is why the tapping on a desk seems louder when the listener puts his or her ear to the desk and listens to the sound through the wood rather than through the air.

HEARING OUR VOICES — Class Activity

Let each student tape-record his or her voice. Then play the recording to the class. Ask how many students think their voices sound different on tape. Tell the class that when we speak, we hear ourselves differently than others do. That is because we hear our own voices as a result of sound waves traveling both through the air and through the bones and body fluids of our neck and head. When we hear ourselves on tape, we only hear the sound waves as they travel through the air.

Name _____

Record Sheet

Listening Through Solids

Work with a partner at a desk.

Follow these directions:

1. Sit and put one ear down on the desk.
2. Your partner should stand about a foot away. Have your partner tap softly on the desk.
3. Now sit up. Have your partner tap softly on the desk again.

Did the tapping seem louder when your ear was on the desk or when you were sitting up?

_____

_____

You hear sound when sound waves travel and reach your ears. Think about the results you got. Do you think sound waves travel through solids? Explain your answer.

_____

_____

_____

25

WHAT DO YOU FEEL?
Class Activity

This guessing game lets children see how their sense of touch helps them distinguish shape, texture, and temperature.

Blindfold three students in front of the class. Next give each child an object such as a chalkboard eraser. Have the students feel the object, describe what it feels like, and then guess what it is. Continue the game with different groups of children. Provide a variety of objects for the class to feel, such as a paintbrush, a mug, a golf ball, an ice cube (on a paper towel or plate), a sock, and a sponge.

Guide the class into seeing that our sense of touch lets us feel various sensations that help us identify an object through its shape, its texture, and its warmth or coldness. Explain that our sense of touch comes from millions of touch sensors located in our skin. Add that there are different types of sensors; each type gives a particular kind of information, such as the hardness, coldness, or wetness of an object.

LIGHT AND HEAVY PRESSURE
Class Activity

Ask the students if they have ever felt an insect on their arms or legs. Ask if the touch felt light or heavy. (light) Tell the class that we have touch sensors just below our skin that send signals to our brain when something touches us lightly. Next, have each student touch his or her hair with a pencil. The students will notice a light sensation. Then have each student lightly touch the hairs on his or her arm with the pencil. The students will feel sensations across the arm. Tell the children that the hairs on our body also help us feel that light of a touch. Explain that we can feel when something touches our hair because each hair has it own nerve ending that detects light pressure.

Next, have each student press one finger on a partner's back. The partner will feel pressure. Tell the class that we have touch sensors deep below the skin that detect heavy pressure. Explain that we can often tell by the amount of pressure whether a person is poking us in a friendly or an unkind way.

PAIN WARNS US
Class Activity

Ask the students if they have ever been burned by a hot iron. If they have, ask if they would purposely touch a hot iron again and why. The children probably will say they would not touch a hot object because they have learned that doing so would hurt them. Tell the class that pain in some ways warns us to keep healthy or safe. Then ask the following questions to illustrate how the sensation of pain keeps us from hurting ourselves:

- A campfire is burning. How do you know when you are getting too close to it?
- It's cold and icy outside. What would happen if you played outdoors in a bathing suit?
- Broken pieces of glass are lying in front of us. Why would it be unwise to step on them?

TOUCHING WITH GLOVES

Class Activity

Do this activity to show that even when our hands are made less sensitive to the touch, they can still help us identify objects.

First, blindfold a student and have him or her wear thick gloves. (If gloves are unavailable, heavy socks will do.) Then give the student a baseball and have him or her try to identify it. The class will see that even though the student's sense of touch is blurred, he or she can still use hardness, weight, and shape as clues to help identify the ball.

Continue the activity with other students. Challenge the children to see how small an object they can identify with the gloves on.

WHAT DID YOU TOUCH?

Class Activity

Have the students keep track of all the things they touch in a day. (Examples: toothbrush, breakfast dishes, door handles, shoelaces) Later, have the students share their lists with a partner. Your class will be amazed to find out that people touch hundreds of things in a day!

"SEEING" BY TOUCHING

Class Activity

Discuss with the class the fact that people who are blind rely on their other senses to make up for their loss of sight. Then do the following activities to show how the sense of touch can help blind people examine the world around them.

- Blindfold a child. Then have the students, one at a time, stand next to the blindfolded child while he or she tries to guess their identity by touching their faces. Continue the activity by blindfolding another child.

- Tell the class about the braille alphabet, in which each letter is made up of a pattern of raised dots. Explain that a blind person can read a book printed in braille by running his or her fingers over the letters. Then let your students try reading raised letters. Get a pincushion and arrange sewing pins on it to form a letter. (Make sure the pins do not go through the cushion.) Blindfold a student and have him or her guess the letter by touching the heads of the pins. Repeat the activity with another student.

Next, let the students make their own letters of raised dots. Give each child a three-inch tagboard square, and have him or her form a letter by squeezing out small dots with a tube of fabric paint (available at craft or fabric stores). Let the paint dry for a day. Afterwards, have one student at a time try reading a letter by closing his or her eyes and feeling the raised dots.

FOUR FLAVORS

Class Activity

Let the class sample the following foods: a salted cracker, a sugar-coated cereal, a sprig of parsley, and a thin slice of lemon. Ask the students to describe the various tastes. Tell the class that our sense of taste comes from taste buds that are scattered over our tongue. Explain that these taste buds detect four basic tastes: salty (like a cracker), sweet (like sugar), bitter (like parsley), and sour (like lemon).

Next, divide a sheet of chart paper into four columns: *Salty*, *Sweet*, *Bitter*, and *Sour*. Then have the students cut out magazine pictures of foods to glue onto the appropriate columns. The children may also write their own food suggestions on pieces of paper and glue them onto the chart as well.

A MATTER OF TASTE

Class Activity

The foods we like or dislike have a lot to do with our own personal preferences and our cultural background. See what foods your students enjoy with this activity.

Give each child a copy of the following list of foods (create your own list if you wish):

apple	chicken	ham	popcorn
banana	chili	lettuce	potato
bean	chocolate	milk	rice
bread	dill pickle	oatmeal	sausage
carrot	egg	pea	spaghetti
cheese	grape	pear	tuna

Then have the students write a number from *1* to *5* beside each food item to indicate their like or dislike of the food (*1* being the least liked and *5* being the most liked). Later, have the children compare their ratings with one another.

NAME THAT SMELL

Class Activity

Prepare for this guessing game ahead of time by setting out plates or bowls containing the following items: a sliced orange, a sliced lemon, a sliced apple, a spoonful of vinegar, a chunk of cheese, a bar of soap, and a sweet-smelling flower. Cover each item with plastic wrap so that the odors do not mingle.

Later, have the students sit in a circle with their eyes closed. Next pass the orange around the circle and have each child take a whiff. Afterwards, ask the students to describe the odor and to identify the item they smelled. Explain that special nerve cells in the nose pick up odors in the air; the nerves send signals to the brain, which then analyzes the smell and identifies it.

Then continue the guessing game by passing the other items around for the children to smell with their eyes closed. After all the items have been used, ask such questions as *What smells were the easiest to identify? Do you think foods are easier to identify than other items, and why?*

TASTE AND SMELL WORKING TOGETHER

Class Activity

Do the following demonstration to show how our sense of taste is enhanced by our sense of smell.

Get three glasses of different kinds of fruit juice, such as apple juice, grape juice, and orange juice. Then blindfold a student and have the student take a sip from each glass while pinching his or her nose together. Ask the student to identify the juices. Next, have him or her sip from the glasses again, but this time without pinching his or her nose. The student will find it is easier to identify the juices when the sense of smell is involved. Tell the class that our sense of taste is affected by our sense of smell. Then ask if anyone has ever had a cold with a stuffed-up nose and found that foods didn't taste as good. Explain that one reason we do not enjoy foods as much when we have a cold is our weakened sense of smell.

HELPFUL SENSES

Discuss the following questions with the students to make them aware of how our senses of taste and smell can help us:

- You smell gas in a building. What might be causing it? (There may be a gas leak.) What could you do? (Tell an adult or call emergency.)

- You wake up and smell smoke. What might be causing the smoke? What might you do?

- You take a sip of milk but find it is sour. Should you continue drinking the milk? Why or why not? (The milk has gone bad and can make you very sick.)

- You just sprinkled something over your cereal. You are not sure if it was salt or sugar. How can you tell which one you used?

© FS-23212 Science Made Simple ▪ © Frank Schaffer Publications, Inc.

Physical Science

Children learn about the world by interacting with their surroundings. Scientific concepts such as energy and matter may not be in a youngster's vocabulary, but they are certainly a part of the child's world. When children play outdoors and feel the warmth of the sun or when they feel the hair dryer blowing against their hair after a bath, they are experiencing how heat energy works. When they see sunlight streaming through a window or look at their reflection in a mirror, they are learning about the properties of light. As children observe and explore their environment, they make discoveries about "how things work." These discoveries lead to a greater understanding of the forces and principles that govern the physical world.

CONCEPTS

The ideas and activities presented in this section will help children explore the following concepts:

- Heat can be produced by various ways such as by rubbing or burning.
- Heat moves through substances. Heat moves from a hotter area to a cooler one.
- Light passes through some materials more easily than through others.
- Light is bounced back (reflected) when it hits an object.
- Light can be split into different colors.
- Colors can be mixed to produce other colors.

LITERATURE RESOURCES

These colorful resources will help children learn more about the physical world.

The Science Book of Hot and Cold by Neil Ardley (Harcourt Brace Jovanovich, 1992). Fascinating experiments, colorful photos, and easy-to-understand text introduce students to the concept of heat.

Temperature and You by Betsy and Giulio Maestro (Lodestar Books, 1990). Clear text and simple illustrations teach children about measuring hot and cold.

Light by Graham Peacock (Thomson Learning, 1993). This colorful book includes instructions for a variety of activities, including a miniature "movie," a kaleidoscope, and a pinhole camera.

Bouncing and Bending Light and *Color and Light* by Barbara Taylor (Franklin Watts, 1990). These intriguing resources encourage children to experiment with light and color.

Light by Kim Taylor (John Wiley & Sons, 1992). Eye-catching photos and simple experiments teach students about how light works.

Heat

Heat is a form of energy. People use heat to warm buildings, cook foods, produce hot water, and run machinery. The sun is the most important source of heat; without its warmth, all living things on Earth would die. As your students study heat, they will see that besides being a useful form of energy, it also is an influential factor in their daily lives, affecting the types of clothes they wear, the foods they eat, and the places they go.

WHAT MAKES HEAT?

Class Activity

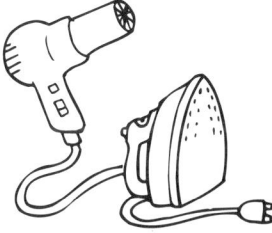

Bring to school a hair dryer, an iron, or other small appliance that generates heat. Show the appliance to the students. Ask the class what would happen if you plugged in the appliance and turned it on. (It would create heat; it would feel warm.) Tell the class that heat is a form of energy. Explain that energy provides power for work. Tell the students that people use heat in a variety of ways at home and on the job site.

Next, ask the students what things at school might generate heat. Write their suggestions on the chalkboard. (Examples: sunlight streaming through a window, a furnace, a hot water faucet, classroom lights, a filmstrip projector, a photocopier) Then assign the following homework activity. Instruct the students to check their homes for things that produce heat and have them make a list of what they find. (Examples: stove, heater, fireplace, toaster, lamp) Be sure to review safety precautions with the students; remind them never to touch anything that might be hot.

Later, have the students bring their lists to school and compile the findings on a sheet of chart paper.

SOURCES OF HEAT

Class Activity

Take your students outside on a sunny day to feel the warmth of the sunshine. Explain that the heat from the sun travels across space and reaches the Earth; when the sun's heat rays touch our bodies, we feel warm. Tell the class that the sun is our most important source of heat; without this heat, all living things would die.

Next, take the students indoors. Then do the following activities to illustrate other sources of heat:

- Have the students rub their hands together; their hands will feel warm. Explain that heat is produced when two objects are rubbed together. Tell the class that before the invention of matches, people made fire by rubbing two pieces of wood together.

- Light a candle with a match. Tell the class that the burning of wood, coal, gas, or other fuel creates heat.

- Turn on a small lamp. Call on a student to hold his or her hand near the lamp but not too close to the light bulb. The student will feel heat. Explain that electricity produces heat; this heat is often put to work in toasters, dryers, irons, and other appliances.

MELTING ICE WITH A FORK · *Class Experiment*

This simple experiment shows how pressure can create heat.

First, give each student an ice cube, a fork, a paper plate, and a paper towel. Instruct the students to lay the paper towel on the plate and to set the ice cube on it. (The paper towel prevents the ice cube from slipping.) Next, have each child put his or her fork on the ice cube and press for one or two minutes. When the students remove their forks, they wil see prong marks on their ice cubes.

Ask the students what happened to the ice. (It began to melt.) Explain that pressing the fork against the ice cube created heat energy, causing the ice below the prongs to melt.

PASSING THE HEAT ALONG · *Class Experiment*

Pour some hot water in a mug and put a metal spoon inside. Call on a student to touch the spoon after a few minutes. (It will feel warm.) Ask the students what caused the spoon to get warm. Elicit from the class the fact that heat was passed on from the hot water to the cool spoon. Tell the students that heat always moves from a hot place to a cooler one.

Next take the temperature of the water and record it on the chalkboard. Remind the class that temperature measures how hot something is. Then record the temperature of the water every 10 minutes after that for half an hour. (The temperature steadily falls.) Guide the class into seeing that heat from the water flows into the surrounding cooler air, and the temperature of the water drops.

HEAT CHANGES FOODS · *Class Activity*

Show the class a pan and an uncooked egg. Ask the students what would happen if you cooked the egg in the pan on a stove. (The egg would become warm; it would change color; we would be able to eat it.) Explain that some of the heat from the stove passes through the pan and cooks the egg. Elicit from the class the fact that heat can change the way foods look. Then do the following activities to show other ways heat creates change in food:

- Place a small piece of chocolate in a plate and set it in sunlight. After a few minutes, ask the class to describe what happened. (The chocolate melted.) Have the students name other foods that melt in heat. (Examples: butter, cheese, ice cream)

- Show the class a slice of bread and a piece of toast. Ask the class how heat changed the bread. (The bread became harder and it changed color.) Have the students name other foods that become harder or change color when heated. (Examples: meat, shrimp, cake batter)

- Show the class some uncooked rice and some cooked rice. Have the students note how much softer the cooked rice is. Then have the students name other foods that become softer when cooked. (Examples: carrot, potato, macaroni)

For a follow-up activity, give each student a copy of *Heat Changes Foods* (page 33) to complete.

Name _____

Heat Changes Foods

Heat can change the way foods look and feel.
Draw or glue on pictures of food to complete the chart below.

Heat makes some foods harder.	Heat makes some foods softer.
Heat melts some foods.	Heat changes the color of some foods.

SOAKING UP HEAT

Group Activity

Show your class a light-colored T-shirt and a dark-colored one. Ask the students which T-shirt they think would keep them cooler on a warm, sunny day and why. Then let the children do this experiment to check their answers. (You will need to do this activity on a sunny day.)

Divide the class into pairs and give each pair a copy of *Soaking Up Heat* (pages 35 and 36). Have the students follow the directions and later let them share their results with one another. The class will discover that the thermometer under the black paper shows a higher reading than the thermometer under the white paper.

Explain that it was warmer under the black paper than under the white sheet because dark surfaces absorb, or soak up, more heat than light-colored ones. Guide the class into concluding that on a sunny day a person would stay cooler in a light-colored T-shirt than in a dark-colored one.

KEEPING HEAT IN

Class Experiment

Show the class a picture of a person dressed in winter clothing. Tell the students that in cold weather we put on extra layers of clothing to stay warm. Explain that the layers of cloth help keep the heat from escaping our bodies. Then do this demonstration to illustrate why this happens.

Get two identical jars with lids and two pieces of lightweight cotton cloth. Wrap one piece of cloth tightly four times around one jar and tape it in place. Loosely wrap the other piece four times around the other jar. Next, fill the jars with hot water. Record the temperature of the water in each jar and then screw on the lids. Measure the temperatures again after half an hour.

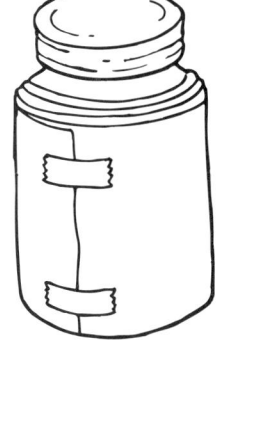

The water in the loosely wrapped jar is warmer than the water in the tightly wrapped jar. This is because the loose layers of material around the jar traps in air; this air acts as an insulator, letting very little heat pass through.

DRESSING FOR HOT AND COLD

Class Activity

Have the students cut out magazine pictures showing summer and winter outfits. Then get two sheets of chart paper and label one *Dressing for Hot* and the other *Dressing for Cold*. Have the children glue their pictures in the appropriate sections. Next, discuss the display with the class. Ask questions to review concepts of heat, such as *Are summer clothes usually light or dark in color, and why? Materials (like fur and wool) that trap air are usually used for winter clothing—why? Do winter clothes try to cover as much of the body as possible? Where could you go on a summery day to feel cool? Where could you go on a wintry day to feel warm?*

Name _____

Experiment

Soaking Up Heat

Question:
Do some materials soak up heat better than others?

Prediction:
Write what you think on the record sheet.

Materials:
black sheet of paper
white sheet of paper
two thermometers
four to eight small rocks

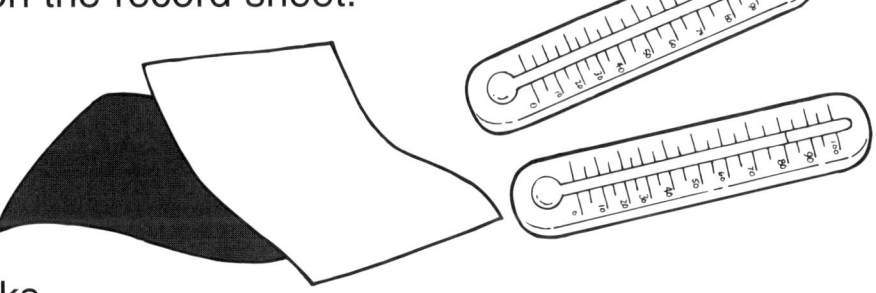

Directions:
1. Go outdoors. Lay the sheets of paper on the pavement in sunlight. Place the rocks on the papers to weight them down.
2. Place a thermometer under each sheet of paper.
3. Check the thermometers after half an hour.

Results:
Describe the results on the record sheet.

Conclusion:
Do some materials soak up heat better than others?
Write your answer on the record sheet.

Name _____

Record Sheet

Soaking Up Heat

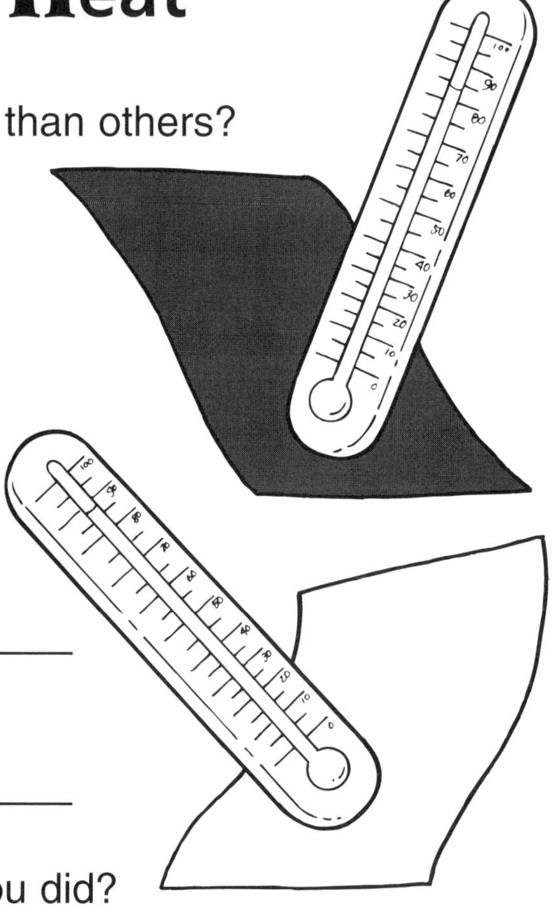

Question:
Do some materials soak up heat better than others?

Prediction:
Write what you think is the answer.

_____

_____

Results:
What was the temperature
under the black sheet of paper? _____

What was the temperature
under the white sheet of paper? _____

Why do you think you got the results you did?

_____

_____

Conclusion:
Do some materials soak up heat better than others? _____

Would dark- or light-colored clothes keep you cooler on a hot, sunny day? Why?

_____

_____

_____

Light

Like heat, light is a form of energy. Plants absorb light and use it to make food, and they in turn provide food for people and animals. Light also enables people and animals to see the world—not only in lines and shapes but in a wide range of colors. The sun is our main source of light; however, light is generated by other means, both natural and artificial. Often, an object that produces light gives off heat as well.

SOURCES OF LIGHT

Class Activity

Show the class a flashlight, a candle, and a light bulb. Ask the students what the objects have in common. (They are used to make light.) Then ask the class to name other sources of light and list their suggestions on the chalkboard. Later, go over the list with the class and have the students identify sources of light found in nature and those created by people. Ask such questions as *What kinds of light do we use during the day? What kinds of light do we use at night?* Elicit from the students the fact that people need light to see and to do their daily activities. Guide the class into seeing that often an object that gives off light also gives off heat.

Next, post a sheet of chart paper in the room and divide it into two columns. Label one column *Natural Light* and the other *Artificial Light*. Then have the class glue on drawings or magazine pictures showing various sources of light. (Examples: sun, star, lightning, firefly; lamp, television set, car headlights)

LETTING LIGHT THROUGH

Class Activity

Call on three students to hold the following items up to the light: some wax paper, some plastic wrap, and a piece of heavy cardboard. Ask the class to describe how much light passes through each material. Tell your students that materials allow all, some, or none of the light to pass through.

Next, let the class examine various items to determine how much light passes through them. (Examples: fabric swatches, containers, toys) Instruct the children to sort the items into three tubs marked *All the Light Passes Through*, *Some Light Passes Through*, and *No Light Passes Through*. Have the children add their own items to the tubs.

For a follow-up, assign *Letting Light Through* (page 38) as a homework activity. The students may check various objects at home by holding them up to sunlight or to a lamp. (Remind the students that they should not look directly at the sun or any other light source.)

Name _____

Activity Sheet

Letting Light Through

Hold up different objects to the light.
Record how much light passes through.

All	Some	None

What does it look like when you look through an object that lets all the light through?

_____

What does it look like when you look through an object that lets only some of the light shine through?

_____

What does it look like when you try to look through an object that lets none of the light shine through?

_____

THE PATH OF LIGHT

Class Activity

Do this demonstration to show that light travels in a straight line. You will need two 3" x 5" index cards, a flashlight, and some tape. You will also need a table that is standing against a wall.

1. Cut identical square notches in the bottom edge of the index cards. Make sure that the notches are in the center of the edge.

2. Tape the cards to the table so that they stand in a straight line a few inches away from the wall. The cards should be about four inches apart from each other.

3. Lay a flashlight in front of the first card. Darken the room and switch on the flashlight. The light will appear on the wall.

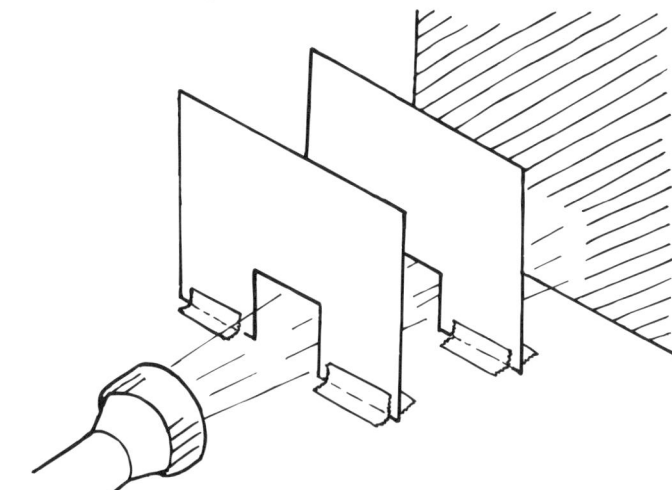

4. Move the second card (the one nearest the wall) so that the notches are no longer in a straight line. Switch on the flashlight. The light does not shine on the wall.

Explain to the class that light travels in a straight line. When the notches were aligned, the light rays traveled through the holes and hit the wall; when the notches were out of line, the light was blocked by the second card and could not shine through the openings.

CREATING SHADOWS

Group Activity

Darken the room and shine a flashlight against the wall. Ask a student to hold a pencil in front of the wall. The class will see the shadow of the pencil on the wall. Tell the students that when light hits an object that it cannot pass through, a shadow forms behind the object. Explain that this happens because light travels in straight lines (see the activity described above) and cannot bend around objects.

Next, divide the class into groups and give each group a flashlight. Instruct the students to hold various objects in front of the flashlight and observe the shadow that results. Have the students look to see what happens when an object is held close to the flashlight and then far away.

Afterwards, discuss the findings with the class: An object that is close to the source of light casts a larger shadow because more light is prevented from passing through; an object that is far away from the source of light casts a smaller shadow because less light is blocked.

REFLECTED LIGHT AND SIGHT

Class Activity

Darken the room and have the students describe what they see. Then turn on the lights and ask the class what difference the light made. (Examples: The room became bright; shapes and colors were visible.) Tell the class that light enables us to see.

Next, tell the students that most objects do not produce their own light. How can we see them then? Explain that light from another source (such as the sun or a light bulb) hits an object and then bounces off; the light then enters our eyes and we see the object. Inform the class that when light is bounced off an object, we say it is reflected.

To show the class reflected light, do this simple demonstration. Stand with a mirror and a flashlight near a corner of the room or near a table, bookshelf, chair, or other large object. Darken the room and shine the flashlight into the mirror. The beam of light bounces off the mirror and is visible when it hits a wall or other object in the room.

MAKING LIGHT BOUNCE BACK

Group Experiment

This experiment lets students discover what kinds of surfaces reflect light best.

Divide the class into small groups and give each group a copy of *Making Light Bounce Back* (pages 41 and 42). Each group also needs a small mirror, a flashlight, two sheets of heavy white paper (such as posterboard), and a sheet of heavy black paper.

After the students do the experiment, let them discuss their results with the class. The children will have discovered that the mirror reflects light better than the other two surfaces. The white paper reflects light well, but not as brightly as the mirror. The black paper reflects very little light. Guide the class into concluding that shiny, smooth surfaces reflect light better than rough surfaces and that light-colored surfaces reflect light better than dark ones.

FS-23212 Science Made Simple ▪ © Frank Schaffer Publications, Inc.

Name _____

Experiment

Making Light Bounce Back

Question:
What kinds of surfaces reflect light best?

Prediction:
Write what you think on the record sheet.

Materials:
flashlight
a sheet of heavy black paper
small mirror
two sheets of heavy white paper

Directions:
1. Work on a table or on the floor. Hold up the mirror and a sheet of white paper so that their edges form a corner.

2. Darken the room. Shine the flashlight on the mirror. Look at the light that is reflected onto the white paper.

3. Put away the mirror. Hold up the second sheet of white paper in its place. Shine the flashlight on it and look at the reflected light.

4. Put away the second sheet of white paper. Hold up the black paper in its place. Shine the flashlight on it. Look at the reflected light.

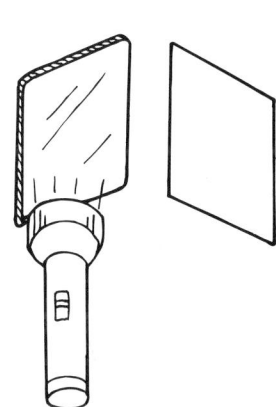

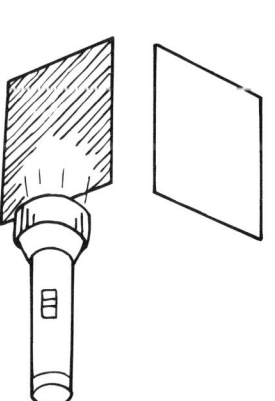

Results:
Write what you observed on the record sheet.

Conclusion:
What kinds of surfaces reflect light best?
Write your answer on the record sheet.

41

Making Light Bounce Back

Question:
What kinds of surfaces reflect light best?

Prediction:
Write what you think is the answer.

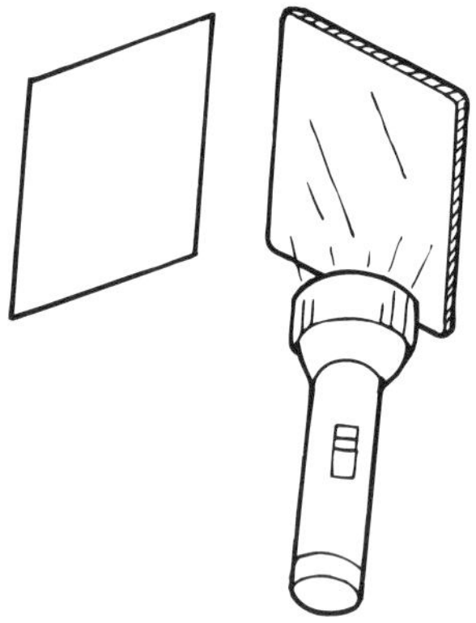

_____

_____

Results:
Describe the reflected light you got:
When you shined the flashlight on the mirror

_____

_____

When you shined the flashlight on the white paper

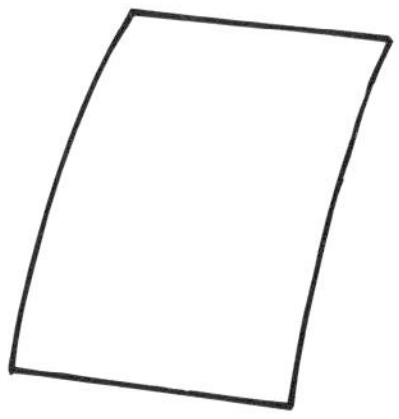

_____

_____

When you shined the flashlight on the black paper

_____

_____

Conclusion:
What kinds of surfaces reflect light best?

_____

_____

LOOK FOR YOUR REFLECTION *Class Activity*

Hold a mirror in front of a student and ask the child what he or she sees. (him/herself) Tell the class that light hits the mirror and bounces away, much like a ball that is bounced off a wall. Explain that the mirror makes a picture because of the way the light is bounced back. Then hold a stainless steel pan (or any other shiny object) in front of a student. Ask if the child can see himself or herself in it. Guide the class into seeing that objects that have smooth, shiny surfaces produce the best reflections.

Next, have the students look around the classroom for objects in which they can see a reflection. (Examples: pencil sharpener, scissors, stapler) Write their findings on the chalkboard. Later, for a homework assignment, have the students make a list of objects they find at home that produce reflections.

FUN WITH MIRROR IMAGES *Class Activity*

Get a large mirror and hold it in front of a child so that his or her reflection can be seen by the class. Tell the class that the picture in the mirror is called a mirror image. Next ask the students if they think the mirror shows the child exactly as he or she is. Then have the child raise his or her left hand; the students will see that the mirror image looks as if the right hand is raised. Repeat the activity with the child and his or her right hand. Ask the students to describe what is happening. (Examples: The mirror image is backwards; the opposite hands appear to be lifted.)

Next, hold a clock to the mirror. The students will see that the numbers of the clock are reversed in the mirror image. Elicit from the class that a mirror image does not show an exact picture of a real person or object; instead, it is reversed (turned around).

For a fun follow-up activity, write some of the students' names reversed on flashcards. Hold up the cards one at a time and have the class guess whose name is shown. To check their guesses, call on a student to hold the card in front of the mirror to reveal the name. Later, let the students write their own words reversed on flashcards for the class to guess. (A child may find it easier to first write his word on a piece of paper, hold the paper in front of a mirror to see it reversed, and then copy the mirror image onto the flashcard.)

COMPLETE THE PICTURE *Class Activity*

Give each student a small mirror and a copy of *Complete the Picture* (page 44). Each drawing on the page shows only half a picture. By holding the mirror to each drawing, the class will be able to see the completed picture. The pictures are: 1. lamp 2. butterfly 3. leaf 4. star 5. flower 6. spoon 7. guitar

Complete the Picture

Color the drawings below. Then hold a mirror against each one to see the completed picture. Write what you see on the lines.

 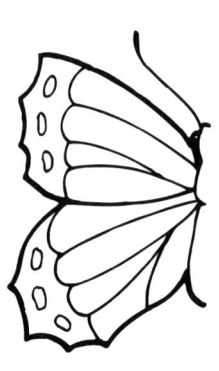 

1. _____   2. _____   3. _____

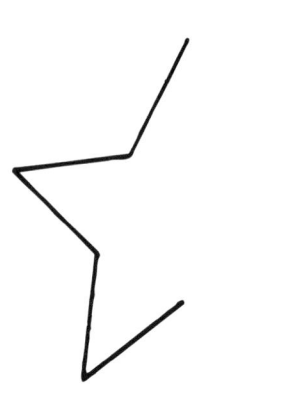  

4. _____   5. _____   6. _____

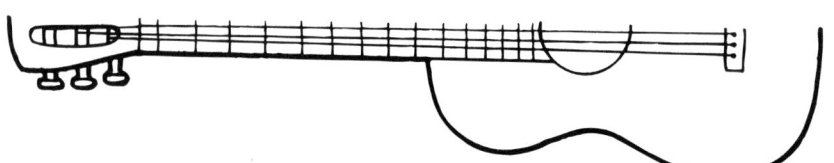

7. _____

Color

Color is all around us, adding beauty and interest to our world. People use color in many ways—to communicate (such as in the use of a red traffic signal to indicate *stop*), to express individual taste (such as in the choice of certain clothes), and to create beautiful works of art. Color also is important in nature; for example, certain animals rely on their coloring to blend in with their surroundings and hide from their enemies. As your students experiment with and observe color, they will discover how colors are produced and how they relate to light.

COLLECTING COLORS — Class Activity

Show your class various red objects (such as an apple, a book, and a crayon). Include things that are both natural and manmade. Have the students identify the color and describe the different variations. For example, one object might be a dark red, another light red, and another orange-red. Tell the class that each color has many different shades—in fact, scientists believe there are millions of colors that can be distinguished!

Next, divide the class into six groups and assign each group one of the following colors: red, blue, yellow, green, purple, or orange. Then instruct each group to cut out magazine pictures showing different shades of its color. Have the students glue their pictures onto chart paper and post their work around the room for a colorful display.

Creating Shades of Color — Art Project

Have the students create new shades of color by mixing paints together.

First, pour different colors of liquid tempera paint into individual containers. Include several containers of white and black paint. Next, give each student a copy of *Shades of Color* (page 46), a paintbrush, a plastic spoon, and a small container for mixing paint. (A deep jar lid will work, too.) Give the following instructions:

1. Choose a color (except white or black). Put a spoonful of that color into a container. Show what the color is like by painting the first square on your activity sheet. Indicate on the first line of the sheet that you have used one spoonful of that color with no white or black.

2. Add one or more spoonfuls of black or white to your container. Paint the second square and record how many spoonfuls of paint you have in your mixture.

3. Continue adding more white or black (whichever paint you chose in Step 2) each time. Paint the squares on the activity sheet and record your paint combinations.

PHYSICAL SCIENCE • Color • 45

Name _____

Activity Sheet

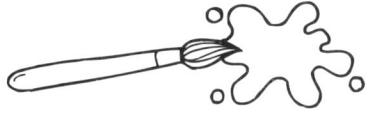

Shades of Color

Create new shades by mixing different amounts of white or black paint with a color. Each time increase the amount of white or black you use. Paint the squares to show your new colors. Record how much of each color you used.

1.
2.
3.
4.
5.
6.

1. _____
2. _____
3. _____
4. _____
5. _____
6. _____

46 FS-23212 Science Made Simple • © Frank Schaffer Publications, Inc.

MIXING COLORS

Class Activity

Let students see what happens when different colors are mixed together. First, fill three tall, clear glasses with water. Add drops of food coloring to make red, blue, and yellow water. Next, ask the students to predict what will happen when you pour some red water and blue water into an empty glass. The class will see that the water becomes purple. Have the students predict what will happen when blue and yellow are mixed, and then call on a child to mix the two colors in another glass. (The water turns green.) Finally, ask the class what will happen when red and yellow are mixed, and have a student mix those colors in a glass. (The water turns orange.)

Tell the class that red, blue, and yellow are called primary colors; mixing these colors produce secondary colors. Then let the students experiment with mixing colored water. Divide the class into small groups, and give each group colored water, a spoon, and several glasses or jars. Ask the following questions to guide the students' experimentation: *Can you make different shades of orange, and if so, how? Can you make different shades of green and purple? What happens when you look at something red through the blue water? What happens when you look at something red through the yellow water? What happens when you mix red, blue, and yellow together?*

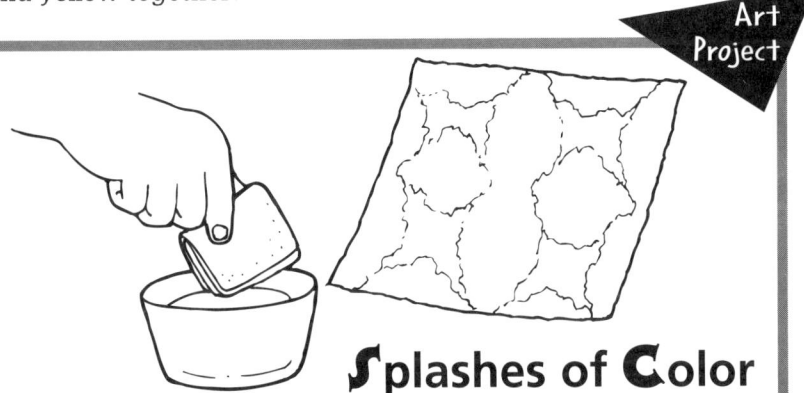

Art Project

Splashes of Color

Let your students dye paper towels and watch primary colors blend to make beautiful designs.

Add red, blue, and yellow food coloring to bowls of water to make concentrated mixtures. Give each student a thick, white paper towel. Show the class how to fold the paper towel several times to make a square. Then have each student dip the corners of his or her square into the primary colors. As the paper towel absorbs the water, the colors blend to produce secondary colors. Have the student carefully unfold the paper towel and leave it on a sheet of newspaper to dry. Your students will be delighted with the colorful designs they produce!

SEPARATING COLORS

Group Activity

This experiment shows that some colors of felt markers are actually made up of more than one color. Pair up your students and give each pair a copy of *Separating Colors* (pages 48 and 49). Each pair also needs five washable markers, a paper towel, and a tall glass. After the experiment is completed, discuss the results with the class. The class will have discovered that the colored strips separated into bands of color; some colors (such as yellow) were made up of only one color while others were made up of a mixture of colors. In addition, different variations of the same color (blue-green and yellow-green) contained different concentrations of colors.

Name _____

Experiment

Separating Colors

Question:
Are some colors of felt markers made up of more than one color?

Prediction:
Write what you think on the record sheet.

Materials:
five washable felt markers
a thick, white paper towel
tall, clear glass

Directions:
1. Cut the paper towel into five strips about one or two inches wide.
2. With a felt marker, color a wide band two inches from the bottom of a paper towel strip.
3. Add an inch of water to the glass.
4. Place the bottom of the strip in the water. Fold the top of the paper towel over the glass to keep it from slipping.
5. Observe what happens to the band of color.
6. Repeat the activity with the other felt markers.

Results:
Describe your findings on the record sheet.

Conclusion:
Are some colors of felt markers made up of more than one color? Write your answer on the record sheet.

FS-23212 Science Made Simple • © Frank Schaffer Publications, Inc.

Name _____

Record Sheet

Separating Colors

Question:
Are some colors of felt markers made up of more than one color?

Prediction:
Write what you think is the answer.

_____

_____

Results:

	Color of Marker I Used	Colors I Saw on the Strip
Strip 1		
Strip 2		
Strip 3		
Strip 4		
Strip 5		

Conclusion:
Are some colors of felt markers made of more than one color?

_____

© FS-23212 Science Made Simple • © Frank Schaffer Publications, Inc.

MAKE A RAINBOW

Take your class outside on a sunny day and have pairs of students do the following activity. Each pair needs a pan half full of water, a small mirror, and a sheet of white paper.

Have the students put their pans of water on the ground. Instruct one partner to hold the mirror in the water at a slant so that the sun shines onto the part that is in the water. Have the other partner hold the sheet of paper so that the sunlight hitting the mirror reflects a "rainbow" onto the paper. The paper may need to be moved away from the pans so that the colors of the rainbow show.

Explain to the class that sunlight is really made up of different colors. When the sunlight hits the water at a slant, the light rays are bent and they split into various colors. In a similar fashion, a rainbow is formed when sunlight passes through raindrops and is split into different colors. Explain that the colors of the rainbow form a band called a spectrum.

COLORFUL BUBBLES

Bubbles have a rainbow of colors when seen in sunlight. The colors are caused by the way the light reflects between the bubbles' thin, soapy layers. Let your students make this easy bubble solution and watch some colorful bubbles float by. The students may work in pairs or in small groups.

1. In a small bowl, mix one tablespoon of dishwashing liquid, one-half cup of water, and one tablespoon of sugar. (The sugar makes the solution thicker.)

2. Twist a pipe cleaner into a bubble wand.

3. Dip the wand into the liquid. Hold the wand near a sunny window to see various colors.

Take your students outdoors so they can blow bubbles in the playground. Have the class watch the bubbles change colors as they float into the air.

A SPINNING COLOR WHEEL

Have your students make a color wheel that demonstrates how white light is made up of different colors.

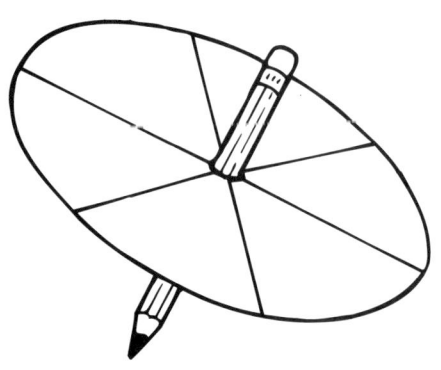

Give each child a four-inch tagboard circle that has been divided into six equal sections. Instruct the students to use their wax crayons to color the sections in the following order: red, orange, yellow, green, blue, purple. Then have each child poke a hole in the center of the circle with a pen. Have the students insert a short, sharp pencil in the hole, place the pencil on the floor, and spin. As the color wheel spins, the colors go around so quickly that they cannot be seen separately; instead the colors appear to blend together and look grayish white.

Earth Science

Children are intrigued by their natural environment. Rain and puddles, wind and waves—children are eager to explore what they see in their world. When given opportunities to observe and investigate their surroundings, children become aware of geological processes such as weathering and erosion. By manipulating objects and materials to simulate natural phenomena such as a flowing stream or a volcanic eruption, children develop an understanding of events in nature. As children grow in their knowledge of "how the Earth works," they gain deeper insights into the nature of the universe.

CONCEPTS

The ideas and activities presented in this section will help children explore the following concepts:

- The surface of the Earth is constantly changing.
- Wind, ice, and water cause changes in the Earth's surface.
- Volcanoes erupt when pressure forces hot, melted rock to the Earth's surface.
- Earthquakes occur when the plates that make up the Earth's crust move.
- Oceans are vast bodies of salt water; they are an important natural resource.

LITERATURE RESOURCES

These appealing resources will help children learn more about the Earth.

Earthquakes by Franklyn M. Branley (HarperCollins, 1990). Earthquakes are presented with simple language and lively illustrations. *Volcanoes* is also available in this science series.

The Ocean by Mel Higginson (Rourke Corporation, 1994). This resource is ideal for students to read on their own. Its easy-to-understand text and colorful photos will fascinate young readers.

Our Planet Earth by Steve Parker (Facts on File, 1995). This question-and-answer book contains interesting questions, clear explanations, and colorful diagrams.

The Sun, the Wind and the Rain by Lisa Westberg Peters (Holt, 1988). This book tells the story of two mountains—one created by nature and the other by a little girl. The captivating story and vibrant paintings describe how both mountains are changed by the sun, the wind, and the rain.

Ocean Day by Shelley Rotner and Ken Kreisler (Macmillan, 1993). Stunning photos and descriptive text help readers discover the beauty and vitality of the ocean.

PHYSICAL SCIENCE • The Changing Earth • Volcanoes and Earthquakes • Oceans •

The Changing Earth

The Earth is constantly changing. Forces such as ice, wind, and water continually attack and alter the surface of the Earth. Sometimes the change is slow and gradual, as in the wearing away of rock by a stream or river. At other times the change is rapid and violent, as in a sudden landslide. As you guide children into observing and studying their surroundings, they will begin to see that the changes in their immediate environment reflect changes that are occurring in the Earth on a much larger scale.

FORCES CHANGE THE EARTH'S SURFACE

Show the class a picture of a new house. Discuss the exterior of the home—the fresh paint, the new roof, and so on. Ask the students if the house would still look new after several years. Elicit from them the fact that the house might need repairs; for example, the paint might be peeling or the roof might be leaking. Guide the class into seeing that forces such as heat, wind, and rain can wear away or damage a house's exterior.

Next, inform the class that forces such as heat, wind, and rain can cause changes in the way the Earth looks, too. Tell the students that just as the exterior of a house becomes worn away after being exposed to the weather, the surface of the Earth is worn away and changed when it is attacked by forces in nature.

SHAPING THE EARTH

Class Activity

Create a bulletin board featuring pictures of various landscapes that show how forces in nature shape the Earth's surface. Beside each picture post a question that the children will find the answer to in the course of their study. Here are some suggestions:

sand dunes—*How were these piles of sand formed?* (wind)

rain on soil—*What can happen to soil when it rains?* (can be washed away)

river—*What is the river doing to the Earth's surface?* (wearing away rock; moving soil and rock)

rock arches—*What caused these rocks to look like this?* (wind and sand)

rocks at foot of a mountain—*Did ice have anything to do with these rocks?* (yes)

glacier—*What happens to the ground when "rivers of ice" flow down a mountain?* (ground gets scraped)

When the class finds an answer to one of the questions, have a student write it on a slip of paper and post it beside the corresponding question.

BLOWN AWAY

Class Experiment

This demonstration shows the effects of wind on soil that is exposed.

Take the class outdoors onto a grassy area. Scoop dirt into a shallow box to make a "hill." Then call on a student to blow at the hill through a straw. The students will discover that dirt blows away easily from the mound. Next, rebuild the hill. This time plant craft sticks into the dirt. Ask the student to blow through the straw again. The mound that has the sticks does not blow away as easily.

Tell the students that wind picks up soil and moves it away, sometimes for great distances. Add that dust storms can result from the movements of soil and other fine particles. These dust storms produce huge, thick clouds of dust that can make it difficult for people to see. Explain that plants (represented by the sticks in the mound) help hold down the soil and keep it from being blown away.

HILLS OF SAND

Class Experiment

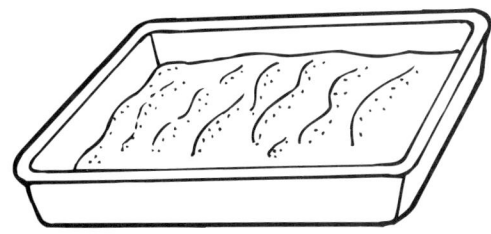

Fill a shallow pan with sand and lay it on a sheet of newspaper. Ask a student to blow at the sand through a straw. The class will see that sand particles are blown away. Ask the students how they think wind affects the surface of the Earth. (It picks up sand, dirt, and other loose materials from one place and deposits them somewhere else.)

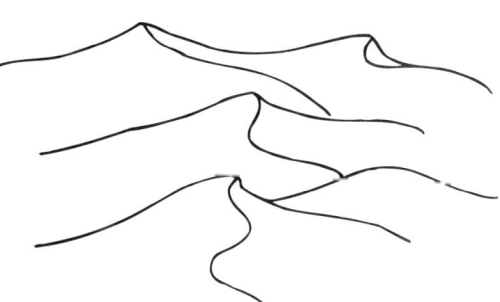

Next, have the student with the straw continue blowing at the pan of sand; the sand piles up into mounds. Tell the class that in sandy places, the wind moves the sand along and builds hills called dunes. Then show the class pictures of sand dunes. Explain that the dunes change shape every time the wind blows and shifts the sands.

BLASTED BY WIND

Class Activity

Show the class pictures of rock arches, such as those in Utah's Arches National Park. Ask the students what might have caused such formations. Tell the class that rock arches are the result of wind. Then do this demonstration for students. Rub a piece of sandpaper against a pencil. The class will see that the surface of the pencil is scraped away. Ask what would happen if you kept rubbing the sandpaper against one part of the pencil. (That part of the pencil would be worn away.) Explain that wind cuts away rock by picking up sand and other particles and blasting it against the surface of the rock.

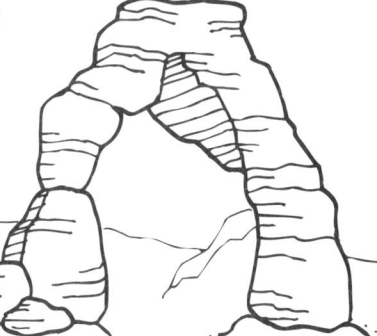

HEATING AND CRACKING

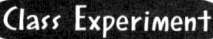

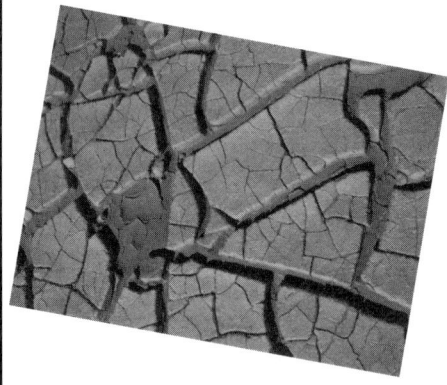

Ask the students if they have ever seen cracks forming along a sidewalk or on the side of a building. Tell the class that the cracks are sometimes the result of heat. Then do this demonstration to show how heat affects rock.

First, get a jar with a screw-on lid. Screw the lid on tightly so that a child cannot open the jar easily.

Ask a child to unscrew the lid. When he or she is unable to do so, place the jar under running hot water. Dry off the jar and then ask the student to try unscrewing the lid again. The lid should come off easily.

Tell the students that the lid expanded (got bigger) when it was heated, making it easier to open the jar. Explain that rocks expand in heat, too, and show examples or pictures of rocks that have signs of cracking. Tell the class that during the day, rocks expand in the sun and contract (become smaller) at night. Explain that this heating and cooling over a period of time causes rocks to crack and break.

RAIN CHANGES THE LAND

Show the class pictures of rain falling. Ask the students to list how rain changes the way an area looks, and list their responses on the chalkboard. If it has rained recently in your area, take the students outdoors to study the schoolyard and then have them brainstorm a list of their ideas. (Examples: makes the ground muddy, makes the roads wet, creates puddles and little "streams")

Later read this poem to the class:

I know it's rained because I see
Puddles and streams all around me.
I know it's rained because I hear
The squish of mud—it's very near!

I know it's rained because I smell
Air that's wet—can't you tell?
I know it's rained—the clues are there,
Just look around everywhere!

Discuss the ways rain changes the land. Then have each student rewrite the poem replacing the underlined portions with his or her own phrases. Afterwards, let the children share their work with the class.

WASHED AWAY

Divide the class into small groups and have each group do the experiment *Washed Away* (pages 55 and 56) to discover how rain can wash away soil and other fine particles. Have the students do the experiment outdoors on a grassy area. The class will discover that the water easily washes away the dirt from the mound that has no "plants" (represented by the leaves or sticks). Discuss the fact that rain pounds away at the ground and washes away soil and other small materials. Explain that plants help hold down the soil and protect it from being washed away easily by rain.

Washed Away

Question:
How do plants affect the way soil is washed away?

Prediction:
Write what you think on the record sheet.

Materials:
two pie plates
dry dirt
trowel or toy shovel
watering can
stiff leaves or craft sticks

Directions:
1. Go outdoors onto a grassy area. Scoop dirt into each pie plate to make two mounds.
2. Insert leaves or craft sticks into one mound.
3. Slowly sprinkle water over the mound that has no leaves or sticks.
4. Slowly sprinkle water over the second mound.

Results:
Describe what you saw on the record sheet.

Conclusion:
How do plants affect the way soil is washed away? Write your answer on the record sheet.

Name _____

Record Sheet

Washed Away

Question:
How do plants affect the way soil is washed away?

Prediction:
Write what you think on the lines.
_____
_____

Results:
What happened when you sprinkled water on the first mound?
_____
_____

What happened when you sprinkled water on the second mound?
_____
_____

Conclusion:
How do plants affect the way soil is washed away?
_____
_____

Which would lose more soil by rain—a hill with no plants or a hill covered by bushes and trees? Why?
_____
_____

WIND AND RAIN TOGETHER

Class Experiment

Review with the class the fact that wind and rain can move earthen materials from one place to another. (See pages 53 and 54.) Then tell the class that sometimes wind and rain can work together to move materials. To show how this happens, do the following demonstration.

Get a 9" x 13" metal baking pan and place a small rock inside it. (To protect the pan from scratches, use a rock that is smooth.) Ask a student to move the rock from one end of the pan to the other by blowing through a straw.

Next, cover the bottom of the pan with water. Ask the student to move the rock again with the straw. The child will find that it is much easier to move the rock when there is water in the pan. Elicit from the class the fact that the water made the bottom of the pan more slippery, allowing the rock to glide along when blown. Explain that rain makes the ground slick, enabling the wind to move rocks and other materials more easily.

THE FORCE OF RUNNING WATER

Group Experiment

Show pictures of rivers to the class. Ask the students questions that will help them study the rivers' characteristics. (Examples: *What color is the water? Is it clear or muddy? Is the river moving quickly or slowly, and how can you tell? Is the path of the river straight or winding?*)

Next, tell the class that a river influences the way the surrounding land looks. Then let the students do the following experiment to find out how a river affects the surface of the Earth. To begin, divide the class into small groups and give each group a copy of *The Force of Running Water* (pages 58 and 59). Take the students outside on a grassy area and have them follow the instructions outlined on their sheets. (The experiment can get wet and messy.)

Afterwards, discuss the results with the students. The children will have observed that the running water carved out a path through the dirt. As the water flowed down the slope, it also carried away dirt and deposited it elsewhere. Tell the class that this is the way rivers wear away the land around them.

The Force of Running Water

Question:
How does a river change the surface of the Earth?

Prediction:
Write what you think on the record sheet.

Materials:
12" x 18" sheet of heavy cardboard
dirt
trowel or toy shovel
pitcher of water
flower pot

Directions:
1. Go outside onto a grassy area. Cover the cardboard with damp dirt. Make some "hills" with mounds of dirt.

2. Place the flower pot under one end of the cardboard to form a slope.

3. Slowly trickle water from the pitcher. Aim for the upper middle part of the cardboard. Observe what happens.

Results:
Write what happened on the record sheet.

Conclusion:
How does a river change the surface of the land?
Write your answer on the record sheet.

The Force of Running Water

Question:
How does a river change the surface of the Earth?

Prediction:
Write what you think below.

_____

_____

Results:
What happened to the dirt as the water flowed down the cardboard?

_____

_____

What do you think happens to the banks of a river as the water keeps flowing over it?

_____

_____

Conclusion:
How does a river change the surface of the Earth?

_____

_____

Some rivers are very muddy. What do you think is the reason for this?

_____

_____

BREAKING UP ROCKS

Class Experiment

Do this simple experiment to show how rocks are sometimes broken apart.

Get a plastic container with a lid and fill it to the top with water. Snap on the lid and place the container in the freezer for 24 hours. The next day let the students examine the container. They will discover that the sides of the container are pushed out. (If the lid was not tight-fitting, it will be lifted off the container.)

Ask the class what happened to the water in the freezer. (It froze; it got bigger.) Explain that when water freezes, it expands (takes up more room); when the container of water was placed in the freezer, the force of expanding ice pushed out the sides of the container. Tell the students when water gets into the cracks of rocks and freezes, the pushing force of the ice sometimes breaks apart the rocks. Explain that the breaking up of rocks by ice often occurs high in the mountains where temperatures drop below freezing at night; the rocks often fall down the slopes and collect in big piles at the bottom.

RIVERS OF ICE

Class Activity

Show the class pictures of glaciers. Explain that these "rivers of ice" are found in mountains. Tell the students that glaciers slowly slide downhill until eventually they melt. Then have the class do this activity to find out how glaciers affect the surface of the land as they move.

Give each student an ice cube, a sheet of wax paper, and a small container of sand. Have the students place the wax paper onto newspaper to protect their work surface. Then give the following instructions:

1. Rub your finger over the ice cube so that it begins to melt.
2. Dip the ice cube in the sand.
3. Rub the sandy side of the ice cube into the wax paper.

The class will see that the ice and sand scrape the paper. Tell the students that a glacier carries rocks as it moves downhill. Explain that the rocks in the glacier scrape against the Earth's surface and wear it away.

Volcanoes and Earthquakes

The Earth is constantly being changed and reshaped by forces such as wind and water. Usually these changes occur slowly and gently, and people often do not take much notice of them. At times, however, powerful bursts of energy from a volcanic eruption or an earthquake occur suddenly and violently, with dramatic consequences to the Earth's surface.

A SPECTACULAR FORCE — Class Activity

Tell the students that the surface of the Earth is always changing. Then show the class pictures of wind blowing or rain falling, and have the class discuss ways in which wind and rain change the way a place looks. (Examples: The wind can blow rocks, dirt particles, and leaves from one place to another; the rain can wash away dirt from an area or cause puddles and streams in roads and driveways.) Elicit from the class the fact that often these kinds of changes are common happenings that pass by unnoticed by most people.

Next, show the students pictures of volcanoes erupting. Have the students describe what they see. Tell the class that volcanoes can cause changes in the way the Earth looks, too. Then ask how changes caused by a volcano might be different from changes caused by wind and rain. Write their ideas on the chalkboard. Guide the class into seeing that volcanoes often get people's attention because of their powerful and spectacular nature.

INSIDE THE EARTH — Class Activity

Here's a simple way to illustrate what the inside of the Earth looks like. Hold an apple in front of the class and tell the students to imagine it is the Earth. Then slice the apple in half. Point to the apple's skin; tell the children that this represents the Earth's rocky outer layer. Next, point to the center of the apple; tell the class that this represents the core of the Earth, an area of solid metal that is surrounded by liquid metal. Finally, point to the flesh of the fruit; tell the students that this represents the white-hot rock underneath the Earth's crust. Explain that the hot, liquid rock (magma) that erupts out of a volcano comes from the mantle.

MODEL OF A VOLCANO — Class Activity

Make this simple model of a volcano to illustrate what is inside a volcano.

1. Punch a hole in the bottom of a clear plastic cup.
2. Insert a straw through the hole. (A transparent straw works the best.) Cut the straw so that it is about the same height as the cup.
3. Take the straw out. Thread a red pipe cleaner through it so that the end of the pipe cleaner just reaches the end of the straw. Bend the rest of the pipe cleaner back and forth to form a mass.
4. Insert the straw through the hole in the bottom of the cup again.
5. Get a piece of cardboard that is large enough to cover the opening of the cup. Cut a hole in the middle of the cardboard.
6. Tape the cup's opening to the cardboard. The bottom portion of the pipe cleaner will extend out of the hole in the cardboard. (This represents the magma chamber located beneath the surface of the Earth.) Trim the straw if it protrudes out of the hole that was punched at the bottom of the cup (the top of the volcano).

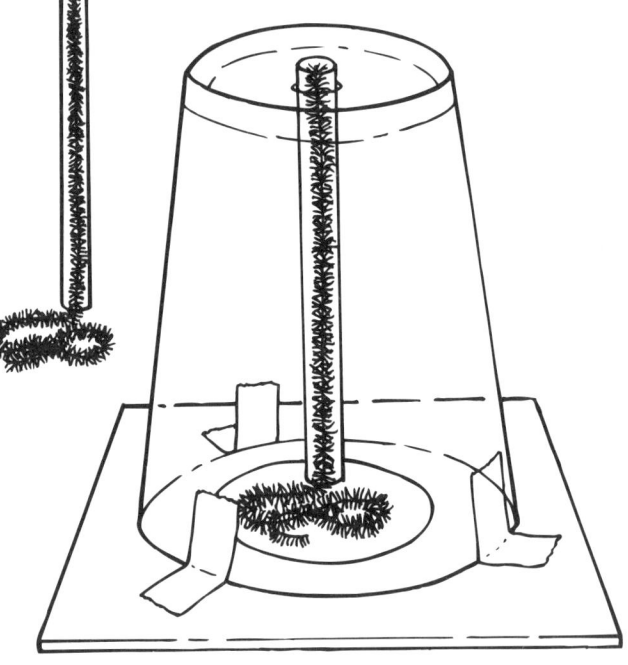

INSIDE A VOLCANO — Class Activity

Show your model of a volcano to the class. Tell the students that if they were able to look through a volcano, they might see something similar to your model. Then point out the following:

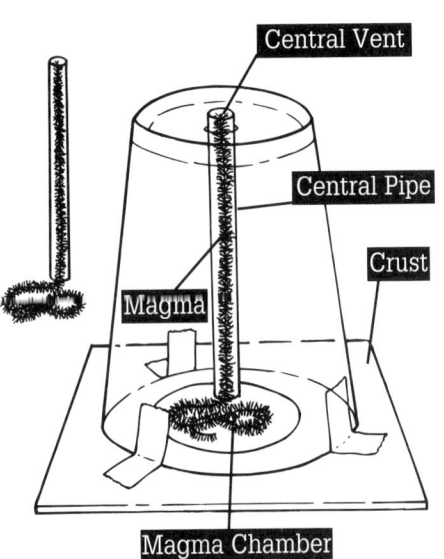

Crust (the piece of cardboard)—This is the outer layer of the Earth.

Central Pipe (the straw)—This is the channel through which the magma rises to the Earth's surface.

Magma (the red pipe cleaner)—This is hot, melted rock. Magma is found deep inside the Earth.

Magma Chamber (the mass of pipe cleaner under the cardboard)—This is located directly underneath the central pipe. Magma collects here, along with gas produced by heat and pressure. When the pressure is great enough, it forces magma up the central pipe to the surface of the Earth.

Central Vent (the hole punched in the cup)—Magma moves up the central pipe and blasts out of an opening in the surface, called a central vent.

PARTS OF A VOLCANO

Class Activity

Give each student a copy of *Parts of a Volcano* (pages 64 and 65). Instruct the class to color the pictures and cut them out. The students then place the outer layer of the volcano on top of the other and staple the two pictures together at the left side. Have the children lift the outer layer to reveal what is inside a volcano.

Later, discuss with the class what happens during a volcanic eruption, and have the students refer to their pictures:

A **magma chamber** lies inside the Earth. It stores hot, melted rock called magma. The magma is filled with gas and is also under great pressure from the weight of the solid rock around it. When pressure builds, the gas-filled magma blasts a path, called a **pipe**, through the rock and escapes to the Earth's surface. The opening through which magma escapes is called the **central vent**. **Gas**, **steam**, and **dust** rise out of the vent into the air. Sometimes the magma also blasts out through other openings called **side vents**. Magma that reaches the Earth's surface is called **lava**.

MAKE AN ERUPTION

Class Experiment

Your students will enjoy helping you make an "eruption" in class. You will need a clear salad dressing bottle, a plastic tub, some warm water, liquid detergent, red food coloring, baking soda, and vinegar.

Place the salad dressing bottle in the tub. Then fill half the bottle with warm water. Add one or two drops of food coloring to the water. Add a few drops of liquid detergent to make the water sudsy. Tell the students to imagine that the sudsy red water is magma deep inside the Earth; the neck of the bottle is the pipe through which the magma travels to the Earth's surface, and the opening of the bottle is the vent from which the magma flows out.

Next, put three heaping teaspoons of baking soda into the bottle. Add about $\frac{1}{8}$–$\frac{1}{4}$ cup of vinegar. The water will fizz, rise to the top, and flow out of the bottle.

Explain that mixing the baking soda and vinegar created a gas called carbon dioxide. The gas expanded, causing the water to fizz and flow out of the bottle. Tell the class that magma contains gas; explain that the gas slowly swells, eventually causing the hot, melted rock to explode out of the Earth.

© FS-23212 Science Made Simple ▪ © Frank Schaffer Publications, Inc.

Name _____

Activity Sheet

Parts of a Volcano

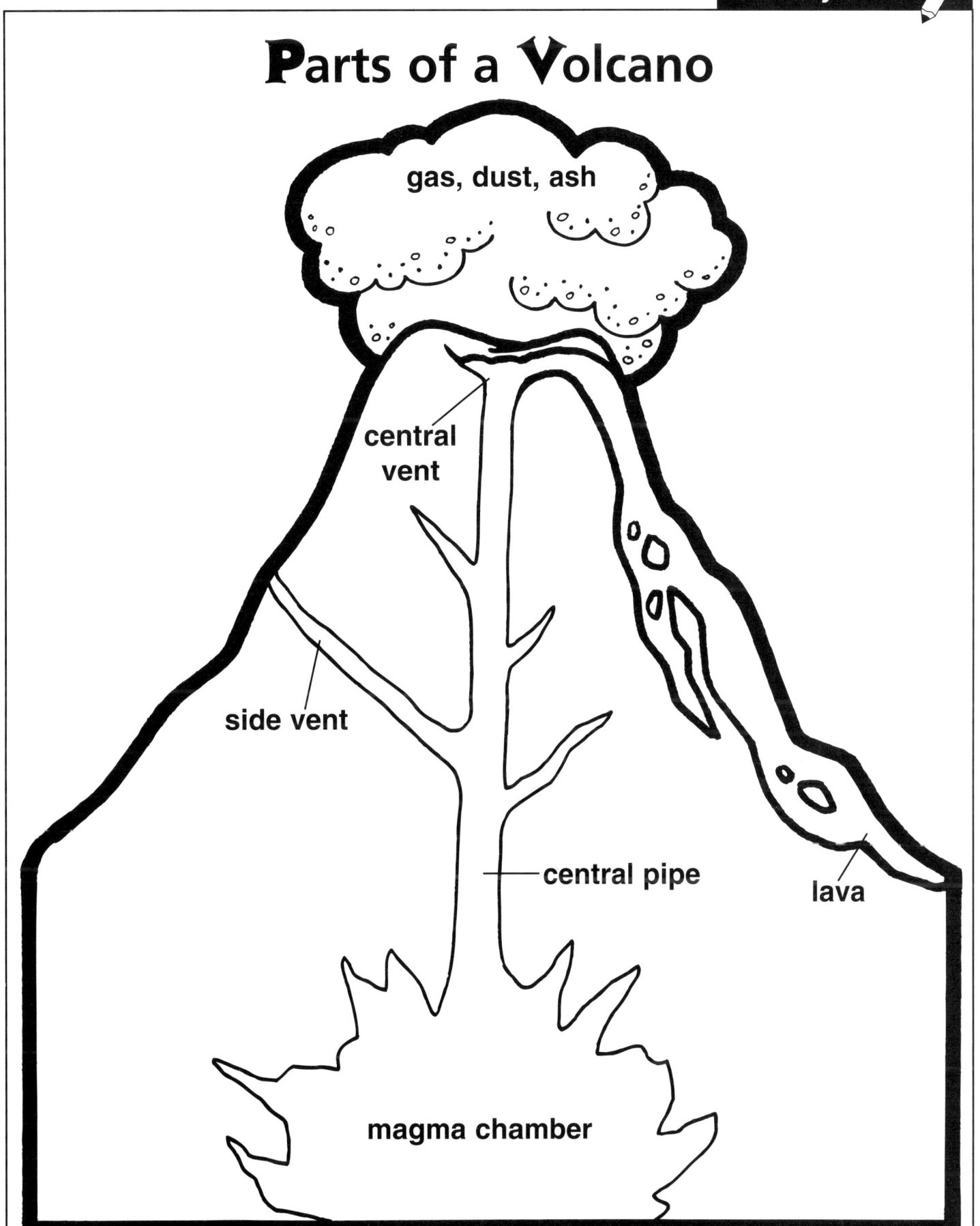

VOLCANOES CHANGE THE LAND

Class Activity

Have the students look through library books and research the various ways volcanoes can affect the landscape. Make a list of their findings on a chart. Here are some suggestions:

- can destroy forests and other plant life
- can cover the land with ash and other materials
- can cause a landslide
- can cause a tidal wave
- can create new rocks—granite is formed from magma that has cooled in the Earth; pumice and basalt are two rocks formed from lava that has cooled and hardened
- can create new islands or mountains

VOLCANOES ARE USEFUL

Class Activity

Tell the class that although volcanoes can be very destructive, causing much damage and loss of life, they can also be very useful. Then have the students research the different ways volcanoes are beneficial to people.

Building and Construction—Rock formed from lava is often used in making roads. Pumice (a light, spongy rock that comes from lava) is used for grinding and polishing metals, stones, and other materials.

Farming—Lava and ash make the soil around a volcano very rich. Farmers sometimes grow crops around volcanoes.

Energy—In some countries, people use the underground steam from volcanoes as a source of energy. This energy is used to produce electricity. In Iceland, hot water created from volcanoes is used for heating homes.

Afterwards, have the students make posters illustrating how volcanoes help people.

MOVING PLATES

Class Activity

Ask the class what an earthquake is. (a sudden shaking in the Earth) Tell the class there are hundreds of earthquakes every day but that usually they are too small to notice. Explain that only when the earthquakes are large enough can we feel them or see their effects. Then use a jigsaw puzzle and a globe to illustrate why earthquakes happen.

Show the class a completed jigsaw puzzle (made up of large pieces) and the box in which it was packaged. Ask what is different between the picture on the box and the actual puzzle. (The picture on the box is one whole piece, but the puzzle is made up of many pieces.) Tell the class that the surface of the Earth is more like the jigsaw puzzle than the picture on the box; the Earth is made up of about 20 different sections called plates. Explain that some of the plates are very large while others are much smaller. Then pick up a puzzle piece and have the students notice the portion of the picture that has been glued on top of it; explain that just as the picture sits on top of the puzzle piece, the Earth's continents and oceans sit on the various plates.

Next, take a globe and section it into large parts with a piece of chalk or a washable marker. Explain that one plate can contain both continent and ocean. Then lift up two pieces of the jigsaw puzzle. Have the students notice that the picture of the puzzle was disturbed because the pieces were moved. Explain that sometimes the Earth shakes because the plates—not the continents and oceans—move.

A SUDDEN MOVE

Class Experiment

Review with the class the fact that the surface of the Earth is made up of plates. (See the activity above.) Tell the students that the plates are moving continuously and slowly. Explain that the place where two plates meet is called a fault. Add that sometimes the two plates push forcefully against each other. Then demonstrate what happens to the Earth when this happens.

Hold up two chalkboard erasers, one against the other, in a vertical postion. Tell the students that the erasers represent two plates. Then push the erasers tightly against each other, at the same time trying to slide one upward and the other downward. The erasers lock momentarily and then suddenly slip.

Explain that in a similar way the Earth's plates lock together when they push against each other. The plates may stay locked for years but eventually slip, causing a powerful jolt.

SHAKE UP!

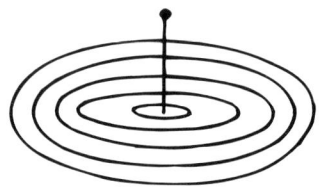

Class Experiment

Tell your students that an earthquake's shaking begins underground. Explain that the ground directly above where this shaking occurs is called the "epicenter." Then let the students do an experiment to find out how distance from the epicenter affects the amount of damage that takes place. Give each child a copy of *Shake Up!* (pages 69 and 70), and have the students do the experiment individually or in pairs.

Afterwards, discuss the results of the experiment with the class. The children will have discovered that the "building" nearer to the source of shaking had the most "damage" (movement of the blocks; blocks falling over). Tell the students that when an earthquake occurs, it sends out waves of energy. Explain that the energy weakens as it travels away from the epicenter; usually, those places nearest the epicenter experience the most damage.

BE PREPARED

Class Activity

It is important for people to know what to do in case of an earthquake. Discuss with your students safety rules that will help them be prepared in the event that an earthquake occurs in their area. Later, have each student illustrate one of the rules, and display the pictures in the classroom.

1. If you are outdoors, stay away from buildings, power lines, and trees. Stay away from anything that might fall on you.
2. If you are outdoors, go to an open space such as a parking lot or a grassy field.
3. If you are indoors, stand under a doorway or get under a sturdy table or bed.
4. If you are indoors, keep away from windows.
5. Keep a supply of bottled drinking water and canned food ready.
6. Have a flashlight, a first-aid kit, and a fire extinguisher handy.

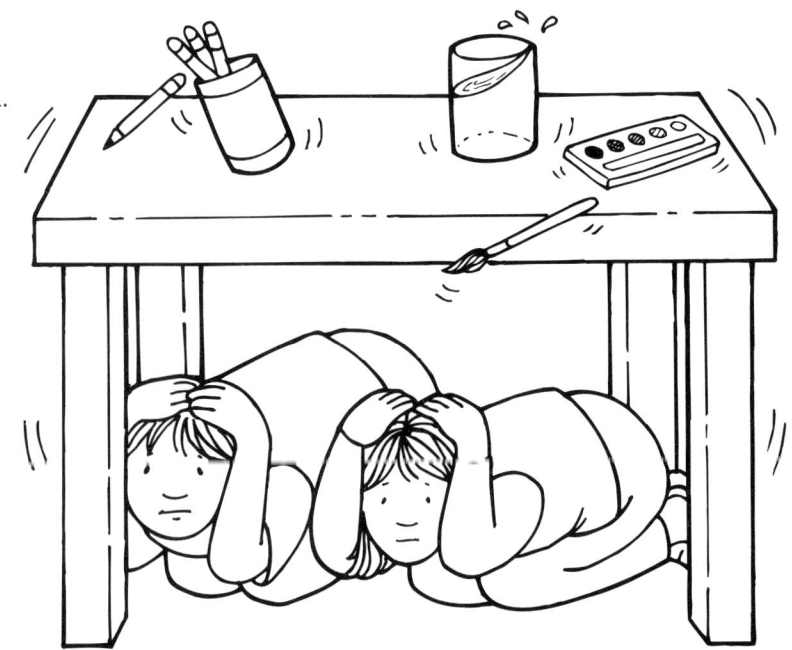

Name _____

Experiment

Shake Up!

Question:
Are places that are near an earthquake's source of shaking more damaged than those far away?

Prediction:
Write what you think on the record sheet.

Materials:
a box (about 12" x 18" on its bottom side)
six small rectangular toy blocks

Directions:
1. Place the box bottom-side up on the floor.
2. Stand two blocks up. Lay a third block across their tops to make a building. Make another building the same way.
3. Put one building about three inches from one edge of the box. Put the other building about three inches from the opposite edge of the box.
4. Start tapping beside one of the buildings. Observe what happens.

Results:
Describe what happened on the record sheet.

Conclusion:
Are places that are near an earthquake's source of shaking more damaged than those far away?
Write your answer on the record sheet.

Name _____

Record Sheet

Shake Up!

Question:
Are places that are near an earthquake's source of shaking usually more damaged than those far away?

Prediction:
Write what you think below.

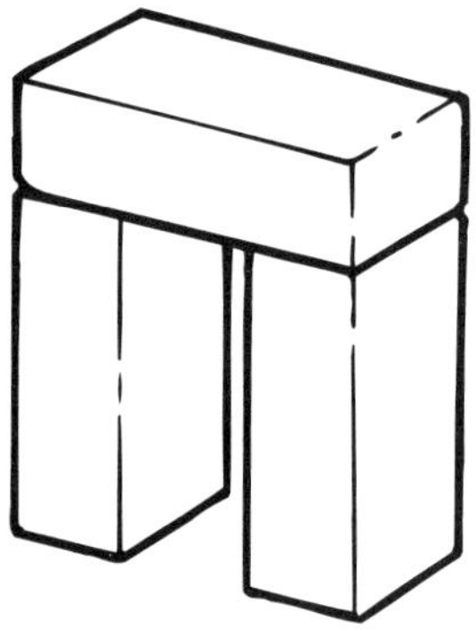

_____
_____

Results:
What happened to the buildings when you tapped the box?

_____
_____

Which building was more "damaged"?
Why do you think this happened?

_____
_____
_____

Conclusion:
Are places that are near an earthquake's source of shaking usually more damaged than those far away?

_____
_____

Oceans

Oceans are vast bodies of water that cover over two-thirds of the Earth's surface. Its waters are constantly moving, energized by the wind and the sun. This movement of seawater affects the climates and also influences the building up and wearing away of land. Oceans provide a wealth of resources for people and are important in transportation and commerce. A wide variety of animals make their homes in the ocean—from microscopic organisms to whales, the world's largest creatures.

SAIL AROUND THE WORLD

Show your students a globe. Ask if they think they can trace a path around the globe without touching land. After your class has had a chance to respond, call on a student to find out. First, have him or her place a toy boat on one part of a coastline. Next, have the student move the boat around the globe until he or she gets back to the starting point. The class will see that it is possible to "sail around the world" because the oceans form one connected body of water.

THE WORLD'S OCEANS

Point out the oceans on a globe: Pacific, Atlantic, Indian, and Arctic. Have the students note that some parts of the oceans are located near the North Pole and South Pole; other parts are near the equator. Guide the class into seeing that although the oceans form one large body, they vary in appearance and temperature depending on where they are located. Tell the class that the surface of the water near the polar regions get so cold that it freezes; the water near the equator, however, can feel as warm as bath water.

Next, give each student a copy of *The World's Oceans* (page 72). Have the children locate the oceans on their maps. Then have the students read their maps to answer the questions. The answers are as follows:

1. Atlantic Ocean
2. Indian Ocean
3. Pacific Ocean
4. Arctic Ocean
5. Answers will depend on where your students live.
6. The waters near Antarctica are cold because they lie in a polar region.

Name _____

Activity Sheet

The World's Oceans

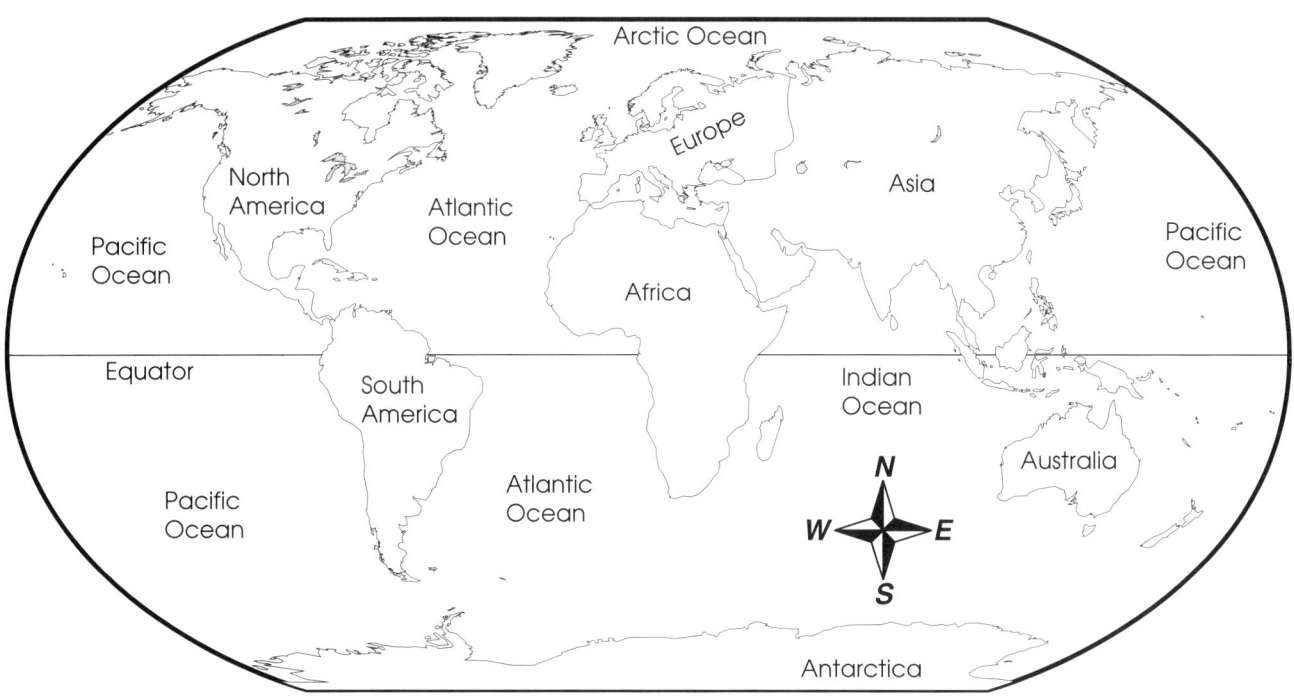

Look at the map. Answer the questions.

1. Which ocean lies between North America and Europe?

   _____

2. Which ocean lies east of Africa? _____

3. Which ocean lies between North America and Asia? _____

4. Which ocean is closest to the North Pole? _____

5. Which ocean is closest to where you live? _____

6. Do you think the waters near Antarctica are cold or warm? Why?

   _____

   _____

SALTY OCEANS

Class Experiment

Ask your students if they have ever tasted ocean water and if so, to describe what it was like. Tell the class that unlike tap water, the oceans are salty. Explain that as rivers flow toward the oceans, they wear away the soil and the rocks they pass over. (See *The Force of Running Water* on page 57.) Soil and rocks contain salts; the salts are dissolved in the rivers and carried to the oceans.

To show how oceans get salty, do this demonstration for the class. Pour a half cup of warm water into a clear plastic cup. Add two tablespoons of salt and stir until it is dissolved. Set the cup in a warm place for several days. The students will see that the water evaporates but the salt is left behind. Explain to the class that when some of the ocean water evaporates in the sun, the salt is left behind. As rivers continually bring in more salt, the seawater evaporates, causing the oceans to get saltier.

WIND AND WAVES

Class Experiment

Fill a glass with water and gently blow across the water's surface. The water in the glass moves. Ask the class why this happened. (Blowing created a wind that moved the water.) Tell the students that when a wind blows across the surface of the ocean, the water begins moving and waves are formed. Then have the class do the experiment *Wind and Waves* (pages 74 and 75) to find out how a wind's speed affects the ocean waves.

Afterwards, discuss the children's observations. The students will have discovered that blowing hard created bigger waves than blowing gently did. Explain that blowing hard caused a wind that moved more quickly; this also increased the amount of energy in the wind. When the wind hit the water, it transferred its energy to the water, causing the water to be pushed upward and form a wave. In other words, the faster a wind moves, the more energy it has; the more energy there is, the higher (bigger) is the wave that is formed.

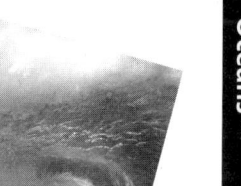

Name _____

Wind and Waves

Question:
How does a wind's speed affect ocean waves?

Prediction:
Write what you think on the record sheet.

Materials:
large baking pan
straw

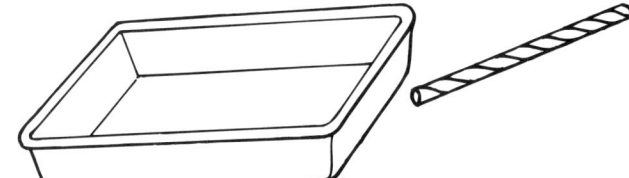

Directions:
1. Fill the pan half full of water.

2. Hold the straw close to one end of the pan. Blow gently through the straw across the water. Watch what happens.

3. Blow harder through the straw. Watch what happens.

Results:
Write what happened on the record sheet.

Conclusion:
How does a wind's speed affect ocean waves? Write your answer on the record sheet.

Name _____

Record Sheet

Wind and Waves

Question:
How does a wind's speed affect ocean waves?

Prediction:
Write what you think below.

_____
_____

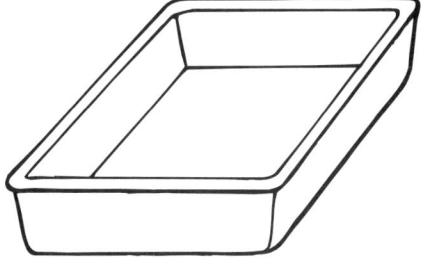

Results:
What happened to the water in the pan when you blew gently?

_____
_____

How did the water change when you blew hard?

_____
_____

Why do you think you got the results you did?

_____
_____

Conclusion:
How does a wind's speed affect ocean waves?

_____
_____

75

WATER ON THE MOVE — Class Activity

Point to a globe and tell the students that oceans are always on the move, traveling around the world. Review with the class the fact that winds are one reason why ocean water moves. (See *Wind and Waves* on page 73.) Then tell the students there is another reason why the ocean is constantly moving.

Point to the equator; tell the class that the water around the equator is warm because of heat from the sun. Point to the polar regions; elicit from the class that the water around these two areas is cold. Then do two experiments to show why differences in water temperature cause the ocean to move.

WARM WATER ON THE MOVE — Class Experiment

For this experiment you will need a large clear bowl, a small bottle (such as a baby food jar), red food coloring, and tongs.

First, fill the bowl with cold water. Then fill the small bottle with hot water. Add red food coloring to the hot water so that it is easily visible. Next, carefully lower the small bottle into the cold water with tongs. Hold the bottle so that it sits at the bottom of the bowl.

Your class will observe that the hot, colored water rises to the top. Explain that this happens because warm water is lighter than cold water. Tell the students that when warm water meets cold water, it rises above the cold water.

COLD WATER ON THE MOVE — Group Experiment

You will need to prepare for this experiment ahead of time by making ice cubes from colored water.

Divide the class into small groups and give each group an ice cube and a clear glass of warm water. Have each group put the ice cube in the water and watch what happens. The class will see that as the ice cube melts, the colored water sinks to the bottom. Explain that this happens because cold water is heavier than warm water. Tell the students that when cold water meets warm water, it sinks below the warm water.

PEOPLE AND OCEANS

Class Activity

Discuss with the class the fact that people depend on the oceans for many things. For example, oceans are used as sources of food and energy; they are also used for transporting goods to and from distant places.

Next, give each student a copy of the activity sheet *People and Oceans* (page 78) and have the class research the different ways people use oceans. Instruct the students to fill in the activity sheet with the help of library books and other references.

Later, have the students share their answers with the class.
Here are some suggestions:

1. Answers will vary. Foods include fish such as tuna and cod, shellfish such as shrimp and oysters, and plants such as seaweed.

2. Answers will vary. Salt is used in various ways, including the following: seasoning food, preserving food, making chemicals, and melting snow and ice from roads.

3. Answers will vary. Countries that have an important fishing industry are located near the sea. These countries include Japan, Russia, China, and the United States.

4. Answers will vary. Recreational pastimes include boating, fishing, swimming, and scuba diving.

MAKE A WEB

Class Activity

Have the class use the information gathered from the above activity to make a web that outlines some of the uses of oceans. This diagram suggests one way your web might get started.

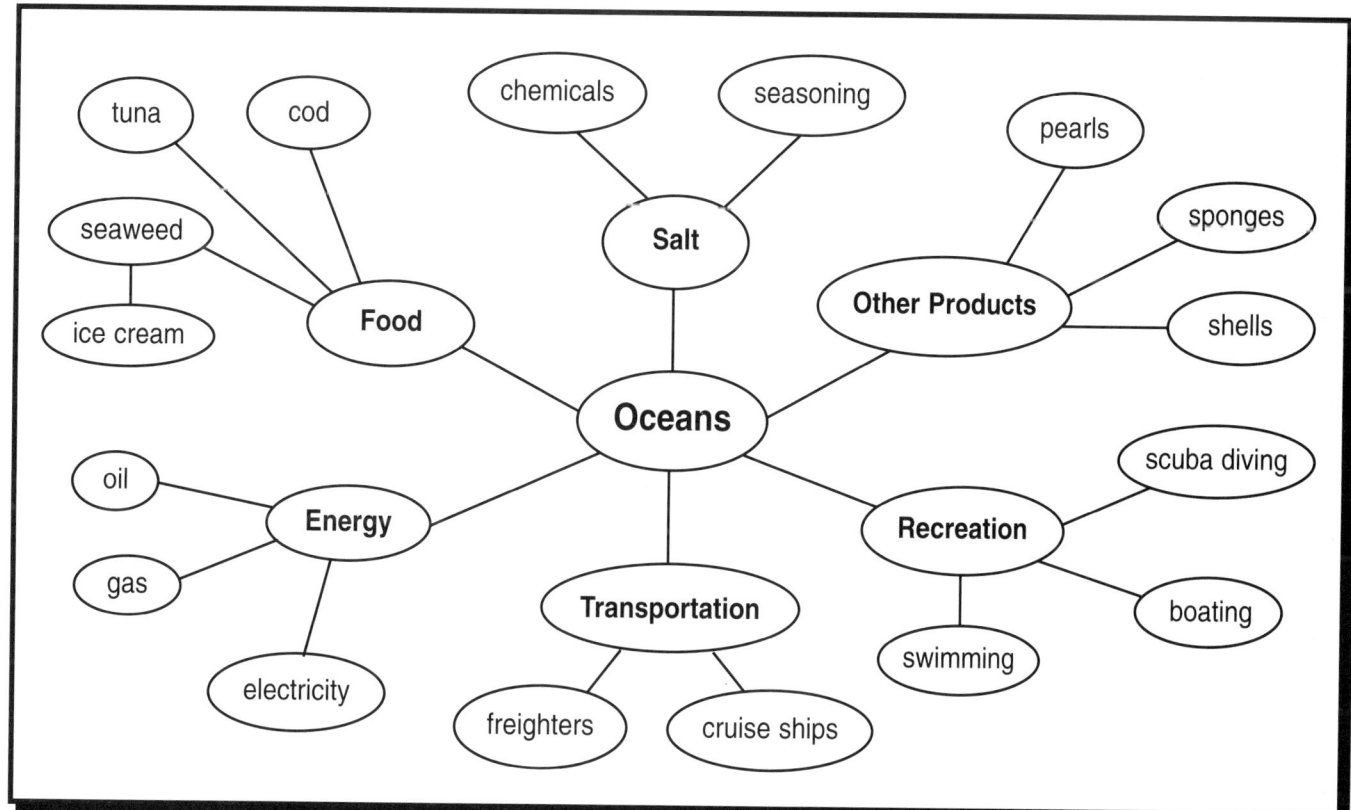

Name _____

Activity Sheet

People and Oceans

People depend on oceans for many things. For example, they get different kinds of foods from the sea. They also get other products such as salt and minerals. People use oceans as sources of energy. Water power is used to make electricity and oil is drilled deep below the ocean. Oceans are also used as "highways" for carrying goods to faraway places.

Find out about the different uses of oceans. Then answer the questions.

1. What are three foods that come from the sea?

   _____

2. Salt comes from the ocean. What are two uses of salt?

   _____

   _____

3. Some people earn their living by fishing. Look on a world map. What is one country that might have many fishermen?

   _____

4. People sometimes relax by going to the ocean. What are two things people enjoy doing in the water?

   _____

   _____